Praise for *Cooking with My Dad, the Chef*

"*Cooking with My Dad, the Chef* is very original and great fun but also a serious read that will get kids into the kitchen and lead to more meals being eaten together as a family. Kids will learn valuable lessons about flavor, choosing ingredients, and nutrition. A fun, wonderful addition to the family bookshelf." —*Jacques Pépin*

"Cooking with my daughter, Sophie, has brought me years of happiness. The Oringer family knows that feeling all too well. In this thoughtful new book, they tackle the difficult task of satisfying kids with deliciousness while navigating the speed bumps of gluten. Truly, a book for how families should be eating today!" —*Bobby Flay*

"From coastal Italian cuisine to Spanish tapas to killer sushi, chef Ken can (and has) done it all at the highest level. Along with his daughter, Verveine, Ken tackled one of his biggest challenges, cooking without gluten. Leave it to the real-deal Oringers to make even the most challenging dishes easy, fun, and delicious." —*Guy Fieri*

"This book is fun for families, young people, and anyone with a big appetite for food and life—it's very digestible (ha!). Ken and Verveine did a fantastic job!" —*Rachael Ray*

"As a chef and the father of two young kids, I've learned that there's no better way to raise good eaters than to get them involved in the kitchen often and early. What a pleasure to see my old mentor Ken Oringer teaming up with the folks at America's Test Kitchen Kids to bring us this fun, usable book packed with smart recipes and techniques designed to empower parents and their children in the kitchen as they explore a huge range of globe-trotting flavors. That it addresses such a common dietary constraint is just the icing on the gluten-free funfetti cupcake. It's no exaggeration to say that I owe my career to the lessons I learned while working for Ken and at America's Test Kitchen. What a culinary dream team!" —*J. Kenji López-Alt*

"One of the biggest joys in life is cooking with family. So this cookbook from one of the best chefs in the country, Ken Oringer, along with his talented daughter, Verveine, is your guide to family cooking. The recipes are not only delicious, smart, and easy to follow, they are also all gluten-free! With great explanations on cooking techniques, equipment, and ingredients, this book will be used by all in your family, so get cooking!" —*Ming Tsai*

"This father-daughter team has created a must-have cookbook for kids of all ages. And, when it comes to food, there aren't many people I look up to more than Ken." —*Nick DiGiovanni*

Praise for America's Test Kitchen Kids

"The inviting, encouraging tone, which never talks down to the audience; emphasis on introducing and reinforcing basic skills; and approachable, simplified recipes make this a notable standout among cookbooks for kids." —*Booklist,* starred review, on *The Complete Cookbook for Young Chefs*

"A must-have book to keep your young adult cookbook section up-to-date and to support the current trend of creative young bakers. A contemporary and educational cookbook that's once again kid-tested and kid-approved." —*School Library Journal,* starred review, on *The Complete Baking Book for Young Chefs*

"Many 11-year-olds like to get in the kitchen. With this cookbook, they can make over 70 delicious recipes. The best part, however, is that the cookbook explains why food cooks the way it does, and it includes science experiments they can do in the kitchen." —*Insider,* on *The Complete Cookbook for Young Scientists*

"A comprehensive cookbook designed for and tested by teen cooks . . . The layout is crisp and clear, starting with ingredients and their prep, with required equipment highlighted for easy visibility." —*Kirkus Reviews,* starred review, on *The Complete Cookbook for Teen Chefs*

About Ken Oringer

One of Boston's most notable chefs and restaurateurs, Ken Oringer has over 30 years of experience in the restaurant industry. In 1997, after working in renowned restaurants from New York City to San Francisco, Ken opened his first restaurant, Clio, in Boston. In its first year, Clio was named "Best Newcomer of the Year" by *Gourmet* magazine, one of "America's Best New Restaurants" by *Esquire*, and also earned Ken a James Beard Award nomination. Since then, he has gone on to open various restaurants in Boston, as well as abroad, to much critical acclaim. Ken's inspiration for his concepts comes from his extensive travels throughout Asia, Europe, and beyond.

Restaurants

Uni (Boston, MA)
Toro (Boston, MA)
Coppa (Boston, MA)
Little Donkey (Cambridge, MA)
Little Donkey Bangkok (Bangkok, Thailand)
Faccia a Faccia (Boston, MA)
Bar Pallino (Boston, MA)

Awards and Accolades: Highlights

James Beard Award, Outstanding Restaurateur - nominated 2017–2020
James Beard Award, Best Chef: Northeast - 2001 winner; 2000, 1999, 1998 Nominee
Food Network's Iron Chef America, winner in the coffee battle - 2008
StarChefs Rising Star Mentor Award - 2010

Library of Congress Cataloging-in-Publication Data

Names: Oringer, Verveine, author. | Oringer, Ken, author. | America's Test Kitchen (Firm), copyright holder.
Title: Cooking with my dad, the chef : 70+ kid-tested, kid-approved, (and gluten-free!) recipes for young chefs! / by Verveine Oringer and Ken Oringer.
Description: Boston, MA : America's Test Kitchen, [2023] | Includes index. | Audience: Ages 8-13 | Audience: Grades 4-6
Identifiers: LCCN 2022051387 (print) | LCCN 2022051388 (ebook) | ISBN 9781954210356 (hardcover) | ISBN 9781954210363 (ebook)
Subjects: LCSH: Cooking--Juvenile literature. | Gluten-free diet--Recipes--Juvenile literature.
Classification: LCC TX652.5 .O75 2023 (print) | LCC TX652.5 (ebook) | DDC 641.5--dc23/eng/20221114
LC record available at https://lccn.loc.gov/2022051387
LC ebook record available at https://lccn.loc. gov/2022051388

AMERICA'S TEST KITCHEN
21 Drydock Avenue, Boston, MA 02210

Printed in Canada
9 8 7 6 5 4 3 2 1

Distributed by Penguin Random House Publisher Services
Tel: 800.733.3000

FRONT COVER
Photography: Carl Tremblay
Illustrations: Gabi Homonoff

By Verveine and Ken Oringer
This book is dedicated to all of the gluten-free kids and families out there. We hope these recipes will open a world of culinary possibilities and help you create amazing memories in the kitchen.

AMERICA'S TEST KITCHEN KIDS

Editor in Chief: Molly Birnbaum

Executive Food Editor: Suzannah McFerran

Executive Editor: Kristin Sargianis

Deputy Food Editor: Afton Cyrus

Associate Editors: Tess Berger, Katy O'Hara, Andrea Rivera Wawrzyn

Test Cook: Faye Yang

Photo Test Cook: Ashley Stoyanov

Editorial Assistant: Julia Arwine

Staff Writer: Chad Chenail

Creative Director: John Torres

Art Director: Gabi Homonoff

Designer: Courtney Lentz

Photography Director: Julie Bozzo Cote

Senior Staff Photographers: Daniel van Ackere, Steve Klise

Photographers: Kevin White, Joe Keller, Carl Tremblay

Food Styling: Joy Howard, Sheila Jarnes, Chantal Lambeth, Ashley Moore, Kendra Smith

Hair and Makeup Stylists: Rose Fortuna, Rachel Berkowitz

Senior Photography Producer: Meredith Mulcahy

Project Manager, Publishing Operations: Katie Kimmerer

Senior Print Production Specialist: Lauren Robbins

Production and Imaging Coordinator: Amanda Yong

Production and Imaging Specialists: Tricia Neumyer, Dennis Noble

Lead Copy Editor: Rachel Schowalter

Copy Editors: Katrina Ávila Munichiello, April Poole

Chief Creative Officer: Jack Bishop

Contents

Getting Started

Hi! I'm Verveine Oringer. I live in Boston, Massachusetts with my dad, Ken Oringer (the chef!), my mom, Céline, my brother, Luca, and my dog, Maple. I've grown up cooking alongside my dad in our house and in his different restaurants. I've always loved being around food, the commotion of the restaurants, and cooking for other people.

A few years ago, I was diagnosed with celiac disease, which means my body can't process gluten, a protein that's found in wheat. I had to stop eating anything with gluten in it, and the gluten-free versions I found just weren't as good. My dad and I started working together on all kinds of gluten-free recipes and I was amazed by how delicious everything turned out. It gave us the idea for this cookbook, so that we could share these amazing recipes with kids and their families, like you! (You don't need to be gluten free in order to make the recipes in this book—they're for everyone!)

Every recipe in this book was carefully tested by my dad and me, by the team at America's Test Kitchen Kids, and by their group of at-home kid recipe testers (there are more than 15,000 of them!) to make sure they work and they also taste great. My hope is that this will become your go-to cookbook for any occasion, that it will teach you something new, and that it will bring joy into your kitchen! Have fun!

Verveine

I'm Ken Oringer, Verveine's dad (and a chef). I've worked in restaurants for over 30 years and I've been cooking with Verveine since she was old enough to sit up on the kitchen counter. When she was diagnosed with celiac disease a few years ago, I took on the challenge of creating gluten-free versions of the foods she was missing—the pastas, waffles, pancakes, and desserts (all the recipes are in this book!). Her diagnosis also motivated both of us to explore foods and ingredients that are naturally gluten free, such as corn-based tortillas and arepas, and rice-based vermicelli noodles and risotto (yes, they're all in here, too). It gave us the opportunity to spend time together in the kitchen—and the inspiration for this cookbook! Whether or not you eat gluten free, my hope is that this book helps you create delicious memories with your friends and family. (And if you are gluten free know that, with the right recipes and ingredients, you can cook anything you want.)

My biggest piece of advice as you start to look through this book: Don't be intimidated. At first glance, some of the recipes might look difficult, but we've spent a lot of time making sure they're achievable at home, whether you're new to the kitchen or an experienced cook. Also, be adventurous! Try a new recipe, taste a new ingredient. You'll be amazed at what you can create, and what you might enjoy eating. You got this.

Ken

How to Use This Book

As you're looking through the recipes in this book, you will see that we've marked each of them as "beginner," "intermediate," or "advanced," depending on the skill level required. We also use symbols to quickly show the type(s) of cooking that will happen in each recipe. Always check with an adult before using anything sharp or hot in the kitchen.

USES KNIFE   USES MICROWAVE   USES STOVETOP   USES OVEN   USES GRILL

Three Steps to Cooking from a Recipe

Whether you're a restaurant chef or in your kitchen at home, the secret to successful cooking is organization. Always start by reading the entire recipe, start to finish—you don't want any surprises while you're cooking! To help you stay organized as you cook, the recipes in this book are divided into three sections: "Prepare Ingredients," "Gather Cooking Equipment," and "Start Cooking!" If you prep your ingredients and make sure you have all of your equipment ready before you start cooking, you won't have to run around looking for the salt while your chicken burns on the stove.

1. Prepare Ingredients

In the restaurant world, we call this "mise en place," the French phrase for "everything in its place," and it means exactly that. Start with the list of ingredients and prepare them as directed: Measure your ingredients; melt butter; and chop, slice, or mince as needed. You can use small prep bowls to keep ingredients organized.

2. Gather Cooking Equipment

Once all your ingredients are prepped, put all the tools you will need to follow the recipe instructions on the counter.

3. Start Cooking!

It's finally time to start cooking. Any ingredients that need to be prepped at the last minute will have instructions within the recipe steps. Don't forget to have fun!

One more pro tip: Clean as you go! Having less clutter around your workspace will help you stay organized—and also means you'll have fewer dishes to wash after you eat. If there's downtime in a recipe (such as during baking), wash your dirty dishes and wipe down the counter. Your future self will thank you!

A note about salt: We use kosher salt in every recipe in this book (except for a few where we call for flake sea salt). If you're using table salt, use **HALF** the amount listed in the recipe, otherwise your dish will turn out way too salty.

Six Kitchen Safety Tips

1. Wash your hands before you start cooking.

2. Knives, stovetops, ovens, and grills can be dangerous. Always ask an adult for help if you're in doubt.

3. Hot stovetops and ovens can cause painful burns. Assume that anything on the stovetop (including a pan handle or lid) is hot. Everything inside the oven is definitely hot—always use oven mitts.

4. Don't ever leave something on the stove unattended. Always turn off the stove and oven when you're done using them.

5. Wash your hands after touching raw meat, chicken, turkey, fish, or eggs.

6. Never let foods you'll eat raw, such as lettuce, touch foods you need to cook, such as raw chicken.

From Chef Ken: What Is Gluten, Anyway?

First things first: **All of the recipes in this book are gluten free, but you do not need to eat gluten free in order to use this book!**

Gluten is a network of linked-up proteins (tiny molecules) found in foods made from wheat, barley, and rye. It's strong and stretchy, kind of like a spiderweb. Gluten is what gives wheat-based foods, such as breads, muffins, and noodles, their structure and their texture.

To make those same foods without gluten, you need to use other ingredients to create that structure. Some important ones are white rice flour, brown rice flour, tapioca flour, cornstarch, and milk powder. Like wheat flour, these ingredients contain starch and protein, but they're *different* proteins from the ones that create gluten.

Over the past few years of testing and creating gluten-free recipes, I've seen gluten-free flours, noodles, pasta, and bread crumbs come a long way. Today, our favorite brands (see page 12) taste just as good as their gluten-containing counterparts. Plus, there are lots of naturally gluten-free ingredients that are also delicious. Think rice, corn (including corn tortillas), fruits, vegetables, beans, meat, chicken, fish, cheese, chocolate, and more.

Our Favorite Gluten-Free Pasta, Noodles, and Flours

Today, there are several brands of gluten-free pasta and noodles that we think are just as good as their wheat-based counterparts. Here's what we stock in our pantry and what we recommend you use.

Gluten-Free Pasta

Bionature Organic Gluten-Free Pasta

Garofalo Gluten-Free Pasta

Farabella Gluten-Free Pasta

Charlie's Gluten-Free Fresh Pasta*

Depuma's Gluten-Free Fresh Pasta*

If you're using fresh pasta, check the package directions for cooking time.

Any of the pasta and noodle recipes in this book will work with an equal amount of wheat-based pasta, if you aren't eating gluten free.

Gluten-Free Ramen

Lotus Foods Organic Millet and Brown Rice Ramen

Gluten-Free Flours

There are many different gluten-free flour blends sold in stores and online. They're made of a combination of ingredients that work together to behave just like wheat flour would. If you look at their ingredient lists, you might see white rice flour, brown rice flour, tapioca starch, cornstarch, potato starch, milk powder, and/or xanthan gum.

The gluten-free flour blends that we use most often (and that we developed the recipes in this book with) are Cup4Cup Gluten-Free Multipurpose Flour and King Arthur Gluten-Free Measure for Measure Flour. In general, we prefer to use Cup4Cup, but you can use an equal amount of King Arthur unless the recipe specifically tells you not to.

In addition to these flour blends, there are other flours that are naturally gluten free. Look for almond flour (made from ground-up almonds), chickpea flour (made from ground-up dried chickpeas), sweet rice flour (made from ground-up rice), oat flour (made from ground-up oats), and millet flour (made from ground-up millet, a type of grain).

Some Favorite Ingredients

Here are some of the ingredients that we absolutely love to cook with—and eat!
A handful of them can be harder to find, but we think they're worth seeking out.
Many can be found in specialty food stores and online. We love having them in
our pantry at home—and we think you will, too!

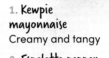

1. **Kewpie mayonnaise**
Creamy and tangy

2. **Espelette pepper**
Smoky and a little sweet (see page 206)

3. **Fish sauce**
A little goes a long way!

4. **Gluten-free tamari**
Salty, umami perfection

5. **Masarepa**
The key to arepas (page 114)

6. **Truffle paste**
Rich and earthy (see page 174)

7. **Flake sea salt**
For sprinkling!

8. **Coconut milk**
Thick and creamy (see page 92)

9. **Miso**
An umami powerhouse

10. **Masa harina**
The base for sopes (page 108) and pupusas (page 116)

11. **Calabrian chile paste**
Just the right amount of spicy (see page 84)

12. **Bomba rice**
The best for paella (see page 96)

13. **Anchovies**
Little fish, big umami taste

14. **Squid ink**
Salty and savory (see page 176)

15. **Carnaroli rice**
A must for risotto (see page 94)

16. **Parmesan**
Best cheese in the world!

17. **Demerara sugar**
Sweet and crunchy (see page 206)

From Chef Ken:
All About Umami

Humans can detect five different tastes: salty, sweet, sour, bitter, and—my personal favorite—umami ("oo-MA-me"). Umami is often described as "meaty" or "savory." And there are a handful of foods that are absolutely full of umami taste. Here are some of my go-tos.

All of these ingredients are full of savory glutamates, the molecules responsible for umami taste. You'll see them in lots of recipes in this book, since I love to add a boost of umami to my cooking whenever I can. Look for a sneaky tablespoon of tamari in Coppa Bolognese (page 58), a dash of fish sauce in Spicy Sicilian Tuna Pasta (page 66), and lots of dishes finished with a sprinkle of Parmesan cheese. Though, Mushroom-Miso Risotto (page 94) might win the award for biggest umami bomb in this book! It features three of the savoriest, most umami-est ingredients you can get your hands on: mushrooms, miso, and Parmesan cheese.

Tomato paste

Parmesan cheese

Gluten-free tamari

Anchovies

Beef

Mushrooms

Miso

Fish sauce

Essential Prep Steps

How to Measure Ingredients by Weight Using a Scale

Using a scale is the most accurate way to measure dry and liquid ingredients, if you have one.

1. Turn on the scale and place the bowl on the scale. Then press the "tare" button to zero out the weight (that means that the weight of the bowl won't be included!).

2. Slowly add your ingredient to the bowl until you reach the desired weight. Here we are weighing 5 ounces of flour (equal to 1 cup).

How to Measure Dry Ingredients by Volume

Dry ingredients should be measured with dry measuring cups (small metal or plastic cups with handles). Each set has cups of various sizes: ¼ cup, ⅓ cup, ½ cup, and 1 cup are standard.

To measure: Dip the measuring cup into the ingredient and sweep away the excess with the back of a butter knife.

Small amounts of both dry and liquid ingredients are measured using measuring spoons.

How to Measure Liquid Ingredients by Volume

Liquid ingredients (such as milk or water) should be measured in a liquid measuring cup (a clear plastic or glass cup with lines on the side, a big handle, and a pour spout).

To measure: Place the measuring cup on the counter and bend down to read the bottom of the concave arc at the liquid's surface. This is known as the meniscus line.

How to Season with Salt and Pepper to Taste

Some recipes tell you to "season to taste" before serving, usually by adding a bit more salt and sometimes pepper. When you finish a recipe, take a tiny taste. Is it bland? Could it use more flavor?

To season to taste: Add a pinch of kosher salt and/or pepper, stir if necessary, and taste again. Repeat until you're happy with the flavor of the dish. Only add a tiny bit of at a time—there's not much you can do to fix something that's too salty or peppery!

How to Crack and Separate Eggs

1. To crack: Gently hit side of egg against flat surface of counter or cutting board.

2. Pull shell apart into 2 pieces over bowl. Let yolk and white drop into bowl. Discard shell.

3. To separate yolk and white: Use your fingers to very gently transfer yolk to second bowl, letting white fall through your fingers.

How to Soften Butter

When taken straight from the refrigerator, butter is very firm. For some recipes, you need to soften butter before combining it with other ingredients. This takes about 1 hour, but here are two ways to speed things up.

Counter Method: Cut butter into 1-inch pieces (to create more surface area). Place butter on plate and wait about 30 minutes. Once butter gives to light pressure (try to push your fingertip into butter), it's ready to use.

Microwave Method: Cut butter into 1-inch pieces and place on microwave-safe plate. Heat in microwave at 50 percent power for 10 seconds. Check butter with fingertip test. Heat for another 5 to 10 seconds if necessary.

How to Melt Butter or Coconut Oil

Butter and coconut oil can be melted in a small saucepan on the stove (use medium-low heat), but you can also use the microwave. If melting coconut oil, be sure to measure the amount before melting.

To melt: Place butter or coconut oil in microwave-safe bowl. (If using butter, cut it into 1-tablespoon pieces.) Cover bowl with small microwave-safe plate. Place bowl in microwave. Heat at 50 percent power until melted, 30 to 60 seconds (longer if melting a lot of butter or coconut oil). Watch carefully and stop microwave as soon as butter or coconut oil has melted. Use oven mitts to remove bowl from microwave.

How to Chop Onions or Shallots

Shallots are smaller, milder cousins of onions. If you're working with a small shallot, there's no need to cut it in half.

1. Cut onion in half through root end, then trim top of onion. Use your fingers to remove peel.

2. Place onion half flat side down. Starting 1 inch from root end, make several vertical cuts.

3. Rotate onion and slice across first cuts. As you slice, onion will fall apart into chopped pieces.

How to Slice Onions

Cut onion in half through root end (see photo 1, above). Trim both ends and discard. Use your fingers to remove peel. Place onion halves flat side down on cutting board. Slice onion vertically into thin strips (follow the grain—the long stripes on the onion).

How to Chop Fresh Herbs

Make sure your herbs are completely dry before you start chopping. And don't overchop—your cutting board shouldn't be stained bright green!

1. Use your fingers to remove leaves from stems. Discard stems.

2. Gather leaves in small pile. Place one hand on handle of chef's knife and rest fingers of your other hand on top of blade. Use rocking motion, pivoting knife as you chop.

How to Peel and Chop or Mince Garlic

Garlic is sticky, so you may need to carefully wipe the pieces of garlic from the sides of the knife to get them back onto the cutting board where you can cut them.

1. Crush garlic clove with bottom of measuring cup to loosen papery skin. Use your fingers to remove and discard papery skin.

2. Place 1 hand on handle of chef's knife and rest fingers of your other hand on top of blade. Using rocking motion, chop garlic repeatedly into very small pieces (even smaller if mincing), pivoting knife as you chop.

How to Tell When Proteins Are Done

The most accurate way to check if a protein (meat, poultry, or seafood) is fully cooked is to use an instant-read thermometer.

To temp: Insert tip of thermometer into center of thickest part of food, making sure to avoid any bones, if present. You can use tongs to lift individual pieces and then insert thermometer sideways into food.

The Difference Between Shimmering and Just Smoking Oil

When you heat oil in a pan on the stovetop, there are two visual cues that a recipe will tell you to look for: shimmering and just smoking. **Shimmering** oil is heated until it begins to move slightly, with little waves on the surface. This tells you that the oil is hot enough for cooking. When oil **just begins to smoke**, you'll start to see wisps of smoke coming up from the oil. (You may need to get eye level with the pan to see this.) Turn on your stove's hood vent, if you have one.

How to Peel, Grate, and Slice Ginger

1. To peel: Place ginger on cutting board and hold firmly with one hand. Use side of small spoon to scrape skin from about 1 inch of one end of ginger, peeling away from you.

2. To grate: Rub peeled ginger back and forth against surface of rasp grater.

3. To slice: Use chef's knife to thinly slice peeled ginger crosswise (the short way).

Favorite Kitchen Equipment

Here are some special pieces of kitchen equipment that we turn to when we're cooking at home. In the recipes in this book, we list alternates whenever possible, in case you don't have one or more of these items in your kitchen.

Spider skimmer

Dutch oven

Cast-iron skillet

11-inch sauté pan

Wok

Pasta roller

Instant-read thermometer

Paella pan

Paring knife

Rasp grater

Chef's knife

Tube pan

Bench scraper

Fish spatula

Kitchen scale

Chapter 1

Breakfast

Blueberry Buttermilk Pancakes

My dad has been making these pancakes for years. They're the perfect Sunday morning breakfast to eat with your family or when friends are over. The buttermilk helps make the pancakes extra fluffy and the juicy blueberries pop in your mouth when you eat them. To cook more pancakes at a time, you can use an electric griddle set at 350 degrees instead of the skillet. We love to serve these with salted butter and maple syrup! For information on substituting gluten-free flours, see page 12.

SERVES 4 to 6 (Makes 12 pancakes)
TOTAL TIME 1 hour

Prepare Ingredients

- 2 cups (10 ounces) Cup4Cup Gluten-Free Multipurpose Flour
- 6 tablespoons unsalted butter, softened (see page 16)
- ⅓ cup (2⅓ ounces) sugar
- 4 teaspoons baking powder
- ½ teaspoon baking soda
- ¼ teaspoon kosher salt
- 2 large eggs
- 1⅔ cups (13⅓ ounces) buttermilk
- 1 tablespoon vanilla extract
- ½ teaspoon vegetable oil
- ¾ cup (3¾ ounces) blueberries

Gather Cooking Equipment

- ▷ 2 cooling racks
- ▷ Rimmed baking sheet
- ▷ Food processor
- ▷ Large bowl
- ▷ Rubber spatula
- ▷ Pastry brush
- ▷ 12-inch nonstick skillet
- ▷ ⅓-cup dry measuring cup
- ▷ Ruler
- ▷ 1-tablespoon measuring spoon
- ▷ Spatula
- ▷ Oven mitts

Start Cooking!

1. Adjust oven rack to middle position and heat oven to 200 degrees. Set cooling rack in rimmed baking sheet (the cooling rack will make sure that the pancakes don't get soggy in the oven!). Place baking sheet in oven.

2. Add flour, softened butter, sugar, baking powder, baking soda, and salt to food processor. Lock lid into place. Hold down pulse button for 1 second, then release. Repeat until mixture is crumbly, about six to eight 1-second pulses.

3. Remove lid and carefully remove processor blade (ask an adult for help). Transfer mixture to large bowl.

4. Add eggs and stir with rubber spatula to combine. Add buttermilk and vanilla and stir until well combined but still lumpy.

5. Use pastry brush to coat bottom of 12-inch nonstick skillet with thin layer of oil. Heat skillet over medium heat until hot, about 2 minutes.

6. Scoop ⅓ cup batter into skillet, using rubber spatula to scrape batter from cup, and spread into 4½-inch circle (don't skip this step!). Repeat 2 more times, leaving space between mounds of batter (you want 3 pancakes to cook up separate from one another).

7. Sprinkle 1 tablespoon blueberries over each pancake. Cook until first side is golden brown and bubbles on surface begin to pop, about 2 minutes.

8. Use spatula to flip pancakes and cook until golden brown on second side, about 2 minutes. Transfer pancakes to cooling rack in oven to keep warm. Repeat cooking with remaining batter and blueberries in 3 more batches. (If pancakes are getting too dark too quickly, reduce heat to medium-low.) Turn off heat.

9. Use oven mitts to remove baking sheet from oven and place on second cooling rack (ask an adult for help). Serve.

From Chef Ken: Pancake Lift Off!

When the baking powder in this recipe meets water (buttermilk is mostly water), it forms bubbly carbon dioxide gas. Those bubbles turn into tiny air pockets as the pancakes cook, making them extra fluffy. The baking soda helps too. When baking soda comes into contact with an acid (buttermilk is also acidic), it forms even more carbon dioxide gas.

Pumpkin Waffles

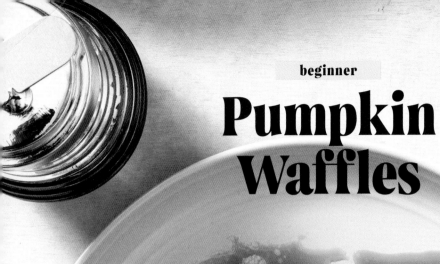

I've been eating these waffles since I was a baby, and I still eat them today. I love them. They taste like pumpkin, but they're not too pumpkin-y. They're doughy but also crispy. I have so many memories of making these waffles, especially of pouring batter into the waffle iron. They're forgiving too (I went through phases of adding molasses to the batter and adding chocolate chips to the little holes in each waffle!). These waffles are great served with maple syrup, bacon, salted butter, or even fried chicken! For information on substituting gluten-free flours, see page 12.

Prepare Ingredients

1 cup (5 ounces) Cup4Cup Gluten-Free Multipurpose Flour

3 tablespoons sugar

¾ teaspoon baking powder

½ teaspoon ground cinnamon
  Pinch kosher salt

1 cup (8 ounces) buttermilk

⅓ cup canned unsweetened pumpkin puree

1 large egg

2 teaspoons vanilla extract
  Vegetable oil spray

Gather Cooking Equipment

▷ 2 cooling racks

▷ Rimmed baking sheet

▷ 2 bowls (1 large, 1 medium)

▷ Whisk

▷ Waffle iron

▷ Dry measuring cups

▷ Fork

▷ Oven mitts

Start Cooking!

1. Adjust oven rack to middle position and heat oven to 200 degrees. Set cooling rack in rimmed baking sheet (the cooling rack will make sure that the waffles don't get soggy in the oven!). Place baking sheet in oven.

2. In large bowl, whisk together flour, sugar, baking powder, cinnamon, and salt. In medium bowl, whisk buttermilk, pumpkin, egg, and vanilla until well combined.

3. Make well in center of flour mixture and pour buttermilk mixture into well. Whisk until smooth, about 30 seconds. Let batter sit for 10 minutes.

4. While batter sits, heat waffle iron. When batter is ready, spray waffle iron with vegetable oil spray. Use dry measuring cup to pour batter into center of waffle iron (use ⅓ to ½ cup batter, depending on the size of your waffle iron). Close waffle iron and cook until golden brown, 3 to 5 minutes.

5. Use fork to transfer waffle to cooling rack in oven to keep warm. Repeat with remaining batter to make 3 to 5 more waffles. Turn off waffle iron.

6. Use oven mitts to remove baking sheet from oven and place on second cooling rack (ask an adult for help). Serve.

From Chef Ken: Pumpkin on Demand

It's really great that canned pumpkin isn't just sold around Halloween and Thanksgiving anymore. Today you can find it in the grocery store year-round, so you can eat these waffles any time you want. The canned pumpkin and the buttermilk make them nice and moist on the inside, but since this recipe uses only ⅓ cup of canned pumpkin puree, you'll probably have some left over. You can save it for another batch of waffles, stir it into your oatmeal . . . or give a few spoonfuls to your dog—that's what I do!

Mochi Waffles with Salted Caramel Sauce

These waffles are so good. They're light, chewy, crispy, and not too sweet. I'm always finding new things to put on waffles—but this caramel sauce is the best. I recommend eating these waffles alongside the Maple Breakfast Sausage (page 48). Be sure to use SWEET rice flour in this recipe, not white rice flour. For information on substituting gluten-free flours, see page 12.

SERVES 4 (Makes 4 to 6 waffles)
TOTAL TIME 50 minutes

Prepare Ingredients

SALTED CARAMEL SAUCE

¼ cup (2 ounces) water

1 cup (7 ounces) sugar

½ cup (4 ounces) heavy cream

2 tablespoons unsalted butter, cut into 2 pieces

½ teaspoon kosher salt

WAFFLES

1 cup (5½ ounces) mochiko sweet rice flour (see note, below right)

½ cup (2½ ounces) Cup4Cup Gluten-Free Multipurpose Flour

1½ teaspoons baking powder

¾ cup (5¼ ounces) sugar

½ teaspoon kosher salt

¾ cup (6 ounces) whole milk

2 large eggs

3 tablespoons unsalted butter, melted and cooled (see page 16)

Vegetable oil spray

Sliced or quartered strawberries

Confectioners' (powdered) sugar (optional)

Gather Cooking Equipment

▷ Small saucepan with lid

▷ Liquid measuring cup

▷ Whisk

▷ 2 cooling racks

▷ Rimmed baking sheet

▷ 2 bowls (1 large, 1 medium)

▷ Waffle iron

▷ Dry measuring cups

▷ Fork

▷ Spoon

▷ Oven mitts

From Chef Ken: What Is Mochiko?

Mochiko is a special type of rice flour originally from Japan, but now you can find it in bakeries, restaurants, and home kitchens around the world. It's often labeled as sweet rice flour or glutinous rice flour, which can be confusing. First, mochiko isn't sweet—it actually doesn't have much flavor at all. Second, it doesn't contain any gluten—it's made from a variety of short-grain glutinous rice called mochigome. "Glutinous" means "sticky" or "gluey," and mochigome cooks up to just that texture. To make mochiko, manufacturers cook mochigome, dry it out, and grind it into a powder. When you mix mochiko with liquids, its stickiness returns, giving baked goods (and these waffles!) structure and mochi its iconic, slightly chewy texture. Another important note: Mochiko is not the same thing as products labeled "rice flour." They're made from other, nonsticky varieties of rice.

Keep Going!

Start Cooking!

1. FOR THE SALTED CARAMEL SAUCE: In small saucepan, combine water and 1 cup sugar. Cook over medium-low heat (DO NOT STIR!) until mixture is deep caramel color, 10 to 12 minutes. Turn off heat and slide saucepan to cool burner.

2. Place cream in liquid measuring cup. Heat in microwave until just warm, 30 to 60 seconds. Remove from microwave.

3. Ask an adult to slowly pour cream into caramel, whisking to combine (mixture will bubble and foam). Return saucepan to medium-low heat and cook, whisking occasionally, for 2 minutes. Turn off heat. Whisk in 2 tablespoons butter and ½ teaspoon salt until well combined. Cover saucepan with lid to keep warm.

4. FOR THE WAFFLES: Adjust oven rack to middle position and heat oven to 200 degrees. Set cooling rack in rimmed baking sheet (the cooling rack will make sure that the waffles don't get soggy in the oven!). Place baking sheet in oven.

5. In large bowl, use clean whisk to whisk together sweet rice flour, Cup4Cup gluten-free flour, baking powder, ¾ cup sugar, and ½ teaspoon salt. In medium bowl, whisk milk, eggs, and 3 tablespoons melted butter until well combined.

6. Make well in center of flour mixture and pour milk mixture into well. Whisk until smooth, about 30 seconds. Let batter sit for 10 minutes.

7. While batter sits, heat waffle iron. When batter is ready, spray waffle iron with vegetable oil spray. Use dry measuring cup to pour batter into center of waffle iron (use ⅓ to ½ cup batter, depending on the size of your waffle iron). Close waffle iron and cook until golden brown, 3 to 5 minutes.

8. Use fork to transfer waffle to cooling rack in oven to keep warm. Repeat with remaining batter to make 3 to 5 more waffles. Turn off waffle iron.

9. Reheat salted caramel sauce over low heat, stirring often with spoon, until warmed through, 1 to 2 minutes. Turn off heat.

10. Use oven mitts to remove baking sheet from oven and place on second cooling rack (ask an adult for help). Serve waffles with salted caramel sauce and strawberries and dust with confectioners' sugar (if using).

Miso-Banana Bread

This extra-moist banana bread definitely has more flavor than your average banana bread. The miso gives it a little hint of salt and umami (see page 14), so it has the perfect combination of sweet, salty, and umami in every bite. My favorite way to eat it is to griddle slices in butter on the stovetop so that they get crispy and buttery on the outside (see page 32 for how to do it). For information on substituting gluten-free flours, see page 12.

Prepare Ingredients

Vegetable oil spray

4 very ripe bananas, peeled

1¾ cups (8¾ ounces) Cup4Cup Gluten-Free Multipurpose Flour

1 teaspoon baking soda

½ teaspoon baking powder

¼ teaspoon kosher salt

1 cup (7 ounces) sugar

¼ cup white miso

8 tablespoons unsalted butter, cut into 8 pieces and softened (see page 16)

½ cup (4 ounces) buttermilk

2 large eggs

Gather Cooking Equipment

▷ 9-by-5-inch metal or glass loaf pan

▷ 2 medium bowls

▷ Potato masher

▷ Whisk

▷ Electric mixer (stand mixer with paddle attachment or handheld mixer and large bowl)

▷ Rubber spatula

▷ Toothpick

▷ Oven mitts

▷ Cooling rack

▷ Cutting board

▷ Chef's knife

Start Cooking!

1. Adjust oven rack to middle position and heat oven to 350 degrees. Spray 9-by-5-inch metal loaf pan with vegetable oil spray.

2. In medium bowl, use potato masher to mash bananas until chunky. In second medium bowl, whisk together flour, baking soda, baking powder, and salt.

3. In bowl of stand mixer (or large bowl if using handheld mixer), combine sugar, miso, and softened butter. Lock bowl into place and attach paddle to stand mixer, if using. Start mixer on medium speed and beat until fluffy, about 3 minutes.

4. Reduce speed to low and add buttermilk and eggs, one at a time, until incorporated. Stop mixer. Add mashed bananas and start mixer on low speed. Beat until combined (batter will look curdled—this is OK!). Stop mixer and use rubber spatula to scrape down bowl.

5. Add flour mixture and start mixer on low speed. Beat until well combined, about 30 seconds. Stop mixer and remove bowl from stand mixer, if using.

Keep Going!

6. Use rubber spatula to scrape batter into greased loaf pan. Place pan in oven. Bake until toothpick inserted in center comes out clean, 1¼ to 1½ hours.

7. Use oven mitts to remove pan from oven and place on cooling rack (ask an adult for help).

8. Let banana bread cool in pan on cooling rack for 30 minutes. Turn bread out onto cooling rack and let cool completely, about 1 hour.

9. Transfer bread to cutting board. Slice and serve or, for an even more delicious option, griddle your banana bread (see photo, right)! (Cooled banana bread can be wrapped in plastic wrap and stored for up to 3 days.)

How To Griddle Miso-Banana Bread

In 12-inch nonstick skillet, melt 2 tablespoons butter over medium heat. Add 2 to 4 slices banana bread and cook until golden brown on first side, 2 to 3 minutes. Use spatula to carefully flip bread. Continue to cook until second side is golden brown, 2 to 3 minutes. Turn off heat. Use spatula to transfer griddled bread to serving plates. Sprinkle with flake sea salt. Serve.

Banana Bread 2.0

There are so many recipes for banana bread out there. And most of them are pretty sweet.

Right, but we love salty and sweet together.

And there's only so much you can do by just adding more salt to a sweet recipe. So I wondered: What if we added saltiness AND umami to banana bread using miso?

It worked great! The miso makes it really special and different.

The miso just brings out so much flavor. I've used it in lots of different desserts, including a miso-caramel ice cream and a chocolate crémeux (kind of like a chocolate pudding) with miso.

Blueberry Muffins

When we make these muffins for my mom, she's the happiest person on earth. We like to use frozen wild blueberries in this recipe, but if you can't find them, regular frozen blueberries will work too. Do not use almond flour labeled "superfine"—it will make the muffins a bit more wet. Be sure to use SWEET rice flour in this recipe, not white rice flour (see "What Is Mochiko?," page 27).

MAKES 12 muffins
TOTAL TIME 50 minutes, plus cooling time

Prepare Ingredients

1⅓ cups (4½ ounces) blanched almond flour

⅔ cup (2 ounces) gluten-free oat flour

½ cup (2¾ ounces) mochiko sweet rice flour

¼ cup (1 ounce) millet flour

1½ teaspoons baking powder

½ teaspoon baking soda

½ teaspoon kosher salt

½ cup (3½ ounces) plus 2 tablespoons sugar, measured separately

½ cup (4½ ounces) plain whole-milk Greek yogurt

⅓ cup extra-virgin olive oil

2 large eggs

1 teaspoon grated lemon zest, zested from ½ lemon

2 cups (10 ounces) frozen wild blueberries (do not thaw)

Vegetable oil spray

Gather Cooking Equipment

▷ 12-cup muffin tin

▷ 12 paper cupcake liners

▷ 2 bowls (1 large, 1 medium)

▷ Whisk

▷ Rubber spatula

▷ ¼-cup dry measuring cup

▷ Toothpick

▷ Oven mitts

▷ Cooling rack

Start Cooking!

1. Adjust oven rack to middle position and heat oven to 375 degrees. Line 12-cup muffin tin with paper cupcake liners.

2. In large bowl, whisk almond flour, oat flour, sweet rice flour, millet flour, baking powder, baking soda, and salt until no clumps remain, about 1 minute.

3. In medium bowl, whisk ½ cup sugar, yogurt, oil, eggs, and lemon zest until well combined. Add sugar mixture to flour mixture and use rubber spatula to stir until well combined and smooth. Add blueberries and gently stir to combine.

4. Spray ¼-cup dry measuring cup with vegetable oil spray. Use greased measuring cup to divide batter evenly among muffin cups. Sprinkle remaining 2 tablespoons sugar evenly over top of muffins.

5. Place muffin tin in oven. Bake until toothpick inserted in center of 1 muffin comes out clean, 27 to 30 minutes.

6. Use oven mitts to remove muffin tin from oven and place on cooling rack (ask an adult for help). Let muffins cool in muffin tin for 15 minutes.

7. Remove muffins from muffin tin and transfer directly to cooling rack. Let muffins cool for at least 10 minutes before serving.

Double-Chocolate Almond Muffins

If you like chocolate in the morning, these muffins are for you. They're really good served warm—the chocolate will still be melty on the inside. (I'll admit: I really like to eat this batter raw too.) If you use almond flour labeled "superfine," your muffins will sink a bit in the center (but will still taste great!). We like the extra-chocolaty flavor you get from using both semisweet and bittersweet chocolate chips, but you can use 1½ cups total of just one type of chocolate chips, if desired.

MAKES 12 muffins
TOTAL TIME 45 minutes, plus cooling time

Prepare Ingredients

1	cup (6 ounces) semisweet chocolate chips
1¾	cups (6 ounces) blanched almond flour
½	teaspoon baking soda
¼	teaspoon kosher salt
3	large eggs
¼	cup refined coconut oil, melted and cooled but still liquid (see page 16)
¼	cup honey
1	teaspoon vanilla extract
½	cup (3 ounces) bittersweet chocolate chips
	Vegetable oil spray

Gather Cooking Equipment

▷ 12-cup muffin tin
▷ 12 paper cupcake liners
▷ 2 bowls (1 large, 1 microwave-safe)
▷ Rubber spatula
▷ Whisk
▷ ¼-cup dry measuring cup
▷ Toothpick
▷ Oven mitts
▷ Cooling rack

Start Cooking!

1. Adjust oven rack to middle position and heat oven to 350 degrees. Line 12-cup muffin tin with paper cupcake liners.

2. Place 1 cup semisweet chocolate chips in microwave-safe bowl. Heat in microwave at 50 percent power for 1 minute. Stop microwave and stir chocolate chips with rubber spatula. Continue to heat in microwave at 50 percent power until melted, 1 to 2 minutes. Stir chocolate until smooth. Let cool for 5 minutes

3. In large bowl, whisk together almond flour, baking soda, and salt. Add eggs, melted coconut oil, honey, and vanilla and whisk until combined.

4. Use rubber spatula to stir in melted chocolate chips and ½ cup unmelted bittersweet chocolate chips until well combined.

5. Spray ¼-cup dry measuring cup with vegetable oil spray. Use greased measuring cup to divide batter evenly among muffin cups.

6. Place muffin tin in oven. Bake until toothpick inserted in center of 1 muffin comes out clean, about 20 minutes.

7. Use oven mitts to remove muffin tin from oven and place on cooling rack (ask an adult for help). Let muffins cool in muffin tin for 15 minutes.

8. Remove muffins from muffin tin and transfer directly to cooling rack. Let muffins cool for at least 10 minutes before serving.

From Chef Ken: Amazing Almonds

 Unlike many gluten-free muffin recipes, this one uses just one type of flour: almond flour. Almond flour paired with chocolate is an amazing flavor combo—kind of like those Hershey's Kisses with the almonds inside. When I was developing this recipe, I played around with different mixtures of almond flour and other gluten-free flours. I kept taking out a flour to see what would happen, and eventually I was left with just the almond flour—it added just enough nutty flavor to balance the chocolate, and the muffins baked up moist and tender.

Monica's Biscuits

Monica Glass is a pastry chef who worked with my dad for many years. She is the nicest person and always saved desserts for my brother and me when we came to the restaurants. She's also gluten free and makes most of her desserts free of gluten—though you can't tell. She invented these tender, buttery biscuits. And now you can try them for yourself! We strongly prefer Cup4Cup Gluten-Free Multipurpose Flour in this recipe—we don't recommend using King Arthur Gluten-Free Measure for Measure Flour because it will make your biscuits pasty. For more information on gluten-free flours, see page 12.

MAKES 6 biscuits
TOTAL TIME 45 minutes

Prepare Ingredients

1¾ cups (8¾ ounces) Cup4Cup Gluten-Free Multipurpose Flour, plus extra for counter

1 tablespoon baking powder

2½ teaspoons sugar

1 teaspoon kosher salt

½ cup (4 ounces) plus 1 cup (8 ounces) heavy cream, measured separately

2 tablespoons unsalted butter, melted (see page 16)

Flake sea salt

Gather Cooking Equipment

▷ Rimmed baking sheet

▷ Parchment paper

▷ 2 bowls (1 large, 1 medium)

▷ Whisk

▷ Electric mixer

▷ Rubber spatula

▷ Ruler

▷ Bench scraper

▷ 2½-inch round cutter

▷ Pastry brush

▷ Oven mitts

▷ Cooling rack

Start Cooking!

1. Adjust oven rack to middle position and heat oven to 400 degrees. Line rimmed baking sheet with parchment paper. In large bowl, whisk together flour, baking powder, sugar, and salt. Set aside.

2. Add ½ cup cream to medium bowl. Use electric mixer on medium-low speed to whip cream for 1 minute. Increase speed to high and whip until cream is smooth and thick, about 1 minute. Stop mixer and lift beaters out of cream. If cream clings to beaters and makes soft peaks that stand up on their own, you're done. If not, keep whipping and check again in 30 seconds. Don't overwhip cream.

3. Use rubber spatula to gently fold whipped cream into flour mixture until small crumbles form.

4. Make well in center of flour mixture and pour remaining 1 cup cream into center of well. Gently fold cream into flour mixture until just barely combined and some crumbs remain.

5. Sprinkle counter lightly with extra flour. Transfer dough to counter. Shape and cut out biscuits following photos, page 40.

6. Use pastry brush to brush tops of biscuits evenly with half of melted butter. Sprinkle each biscuit with a bit of flake sea salt.

7. Place baking sheet in oven. Bake until biscuits are puffed and golden, 12 to 14 minutes.

8. Use oven mitts to remove baking sheet from oven and place on cooling rack (ask an adult for help). Carefully brush biscuits with remaining melted butter. Let cool for 5 minutes. Serve warm.

Keep Going!

How to Shape Biscuits

1. Gently pat dough into 8-by-5-inch rectangle, about ¾ inch thick, using bench scraper to help form tidy rectangle.

2. Use 2½-inch round cutter to cut out 6 biscuits. Place biscuits on parchment-lined baking sheet, leaving space between biscuits.

From Chef Ken: Better Biscuits

There are two things that make Monica's biscuits special and amazing. First, the whipped cream. Gently folding airy whipped cream into the dough gives the finished biscuits a light, fluffy texture. Second, the sprinkle of flake sea salt on top of each biscuit. Biscuits can be on the bland side, so a jolt of salt acts as a flavor enhancer and it also adds pops of crunchy texture. It's a nice contrast to the fluffy, tender biscuit.

Creamy French Scrambled Eggs

I come from a family that is very particular about their eggs, but these creamy, runny eggs are always an exception: We all love them (except my dad, but he doesn't like any eggs). The first time we tried them was in Paris, when we put them in a croissant and fell in love. Since then, we've always taken a little extra time to get the texture just right. When my brother and I would order these eggs at my dad's restaurant Uni, we would tell the server to "make sure they are so runny you can drink them with a straw!"

Prepare Ingredients

4	large eggs
½	teaspoon kosher salt
	Pinch pepper
4	tablespoons unsalted butter, cut into 1-tablespoon pieces

Gather Cooking Equipment

▷ Medium bowl

▷ Fork

▷ Small saucepan

▷ Whisk

▷ Serving plates

Start Cooking!

1. In medium bowl, use fork to beat eggs, salt, and pepper until well combined and uniform in color (make sure to use a fork, not a whisk!).

2. In small saucepan, melt 1 tablespoon butter over low heat. Slide saucepan off heat. Add eggs and slowly whisk, moving whisk around entire bottom of saucepan and making sure to get into all corners.

3. Return saucepan to low heat and cook, whisking constantly, until eggs just start to thicken and come together, about 5 minutes.

4. As soon as eggs start to thicken, whisk a bit more vigorously. Once eggs are thick, turn off heat and slide saucepan to cool burner. Continue to whisk vigorously until you can see bottom center of saucepan and whisk leaves trail, about 1 minute (see photo, below).

5. Add remaining 3 tablespoons butter and whisk until butter is melted—eggs should look like porridge. Transfer eggs to serving plates and serve immediately.

How to Make Creamy Eggs

As soon as eggs are thick, turn off heat and slide saucepan to cool burner. Continue to whisk vigorously until you can see bottom center of saucepan and whisk leaves trail, about 1 minute.

From Chef Ken: Excellent Eggs

This technique takes a few more minutes than just quickly cooking eggs in a hot skillet, but the results are worth it. This is how I was trained to cook eggs in French kitchens when I was a young cook. It's how I cook eggs in my restaurants. And it's how I make eggs for Verveine and her brother, Luca. The key is to cook them slowly, over low heat, and to whisk, whisk, whisk. All that whisking creates tiny curds that cook up rich and creamy—well, the butter helps, too. Here's a fun fact: I don't actually like eggs. I love cooking them, but they're the one thing I just can't eat.

Fluffy Egg Bites

Inspired by the egg sandwich served at the Boston institution Flour Bakery + Cafe, these fluffy egg bites can be enjoyed on their own, in egg sandwiches, or on toasted English muffins. Because they're made with whipped egg whites, they're similar to a soufflé and have a unique and delicious texture. Go try them for yourself! Chiles contain a compound called capsaicin that makes them spicy. To make sure you do not get it on your skin or in your eyes, always wear disposable gloves when working with chiles (don't touch your eyes, nose, or mouth) and clean all tools and surfaces once you're done.

Prepare Ingredients

1	tablespoon extra-virgin olive oil
2	large eggs, separated (see page 16)
¼	teaspoon kosher salt
1	tablespoon finely chopped jalapeño chile
1	scallion, dark-green part only, chopped
⅓	cup shredded sharp cheddar cheese (1½ ounces)

Gather Cooking Equipment

▷ Pastry brush

▷ 24-cup mini-muffin tin

▷ Medium bowl

▷ Whisk

▷ Liquid measuring cup

▷ Oven mitts

▷ Cooling rack

▷ Fork

▷ Serving plates

Start Cooking!

1. Adjust oven rack to middle position and heat oven to 350 degrees. Use pastry brush to paint insides of 8 center cups of 24-cup mini-muffin tin with oil.

2. In medium bowl, vigorously whisk egg whites until fluffy, about 1 minute (this should be a bit of a workout—see photo, below). Add egg yolks and salt and whisk until combined, about 30 seconds. Pour egg mixture into liquid measuring cup.

3. Pour egg mixture into greased muffins cups, dividing evenly among 8 greased cups (cups should be almost full). Sprinkle jalapeño and scallion green evenly over egg mixture in each cup, then sprinkle cheddar on top.

4. Place muffin tin in oven. Bake until lightly browned and puffy, about 10 minutes.

5. Use oven mitts to remove muffin tin from oven and place on cooling rack (ask an adult for help). Use fork to carefully remove egg bites from muffin tin and transfer to serving plates (muffin tin will be HOT!). Serve immediately.

How to Whisk Egg Whites

In medium bowl, vigorously whisk egg whites, moving whisk side to side, until fluffy, about 1 minute.

Turkey Hash

I've always been a diner person. I love seeing the old photos, the red diner chairs, and the regulars who order the same thing every day. I always order the gluten-free pancakes and turkey hash. This turkey hash is inspired by just that. It's easy to make at home, so you can bring the diner to you! Potatoes can be difficult to prep—because they're starchy, they can easily stick to your knife. Be sure to ask an adult to help you cut them. You can substitute leftover cooked chicken for the turkey. Serve this hash alongside eggs or on its own.

Prepare Ingredients

- 1½ pounds Yukon Gold potatoes, peeled and cut into 1-inch pieces
- 1 teaspoon plus 2 teaspoons kosher salt, measured separately
- 3 tablespoons unsalted butter
- 2 tablespoons extra-virgin olive oil
- 1 onion, peeled and chopped fine (see page 17)
- 1 green bell pepper, stemmed, seeded, and chopped fine
- 1 garlic clove, peeled and minced (see page 17)
- 1 teaspoon pepper
- 8 ounces leftover cooked turkey, cut into ½-inch chunks
- ¾ cup chicken broth
- 3 tablespoons chopped fresh cilantro (see page 17)
- 1 teaspoon paprika
- ½–1 teaspoon hot sauce

Gather Cooking Equipment

- ▷ Large saucepan
- ▷ Ruler
- ▷ Fork
- ▷ Colander
- ▷ 12-inch cast-iron skillet or 12-inch nonstick skillet
- ▷ Wooden spoon

Start Cooking!

1. Place potatoes in large saucepan. Add cold water to cover by 1 inch. Add 1 teaspoon salt. Bring to a boil over medium-high heat. Reduce heat to medium and cook until very tender, 15 to 17 minutes (you can check for doneness by piercing potatoes with fork—fork should slide easily in and out of potato; ask an adult for help). Turn off heat.

2. Place colander in sink. Ask an adult to drain potatoes in colander.

3. In 12-inch cast-iron skillet, heat butter and oil over medium heat until butter is melted. Add onion, bell pepper, garlic, pepper, and remaining 2 teaspoons salt. Cook, stirring occasionally with wooden spoon, until softened and lightly browned, 5 to 7 minutes.

4. Add drained potatoes and cook, stirring occasionally, until potatoes start to brown, about 10 minutes.

5. Add turkey, broth, cilantro, paprika, and hot sauce. Cook, stirring occasionally, until liquid has evaporated and potatoes are crisped and browned, 8 to 10 minutes. Turn off heat. Serve.

From Chef Ken: Perfect Potatoes

I love when potatoes start to fall apart as you cook them and get that really crispy crust on the outside but stay creamy on the inside. It's just the perfect combination of textures. The trick is to cook the potatoes twice. First you boil them. This softens the potatoes all the way through and creates that creamy interior. Then you fry them in a skillet, where the hot butter and oil gives the outsides a perfectly browned, crispy crust.

Maple Breakfast Sausage

 These sausages are such a delicious and easy breakfast food. To add a cherry on top, my dog's name is Maple, and while others in my family might disagree, I like to think she's named after one of my favorite breakfast foods: these sausages. They're a crowd-pleaser. They have lots of spices and flavor but are balanced with a sweetness that makes them perfect for breakfast. Pork is the most traditional meat to use in this sausage, but you can also use ground turkey, ground chicken, or ground beef.

SERVES 4 (Makes 8 patties)
TOTAL TIME 30 minutes

Prepare Ingredients

1	pound ground pork
2	tablespoons maple syrup
1	tablespoon chopped fresh sage (see page 17)
1	teaspoon kosher salt
1	teaspoon paprika
½	teaspoon Old Bay seasoning
½	teaspoon ground fennel
½	teaspoon garlic powder
½	teaspoon pepper
¼	teaspoon cayenne pepper
1	tablespoon plus 2 tablespoons extra-virgin olive oil, measured separately

Gather Cooking Equipment

▷ Medium bowl

▷ Ruler

▷ Large plate

▷ 12-inch nonstick skillet

▷ Spatula

▷ Instant-read thermometer

▷ Serving platter

Start Cooking!

1. In medium bowl, combine pork, maple syrup, sage, salt, paprika, Old Bay, fennel, garlic powder, pepper, cayenne, and 1 tablespoon oil. Use your hands to mix until well combined.

2. Lightly wet your hands with cold water and use them to divide pork mixture into 8 equal portions. Roll each portion into ball. Flatten each ball into circle that measures 3½ inches wide and ¼ inch thick. Place patties on large plate. Wash your hands.

3. In 12-inch nonstick skillet, heat remaining 2 tablespoons oil over medium heat until shimmering, about 2 minutes (oil should be hot but not smoking; see page 18). Swirl skillet to coat evenly with oil.

4. Place 4 patties in skillet and cook until browned, about 2 minutes. Use spatula to flip patties and continue to cook until browned on second side and patties register 165 degrees on instant-read thermometer (see page 18), about 2 minutes.

5. Transfer to serving platter. Repeat cooking with remaining 4 patties and transfer to serving platter. Turn off heat. Serve.

What's in a Name?

Here's a culinary mystery for you: What makes breakfast sausage, breakfast sausage? How is it different from, say, Italian sausage or bratwurst?

Great question. I think it's the flavorings. For some reason, sage is always in breakfast sausage. And there's usually some maple syrup in there too. You don't see that in other kinds of sausage.

And I think breakfast sausage is the only kind of sausage you see in both links and flat patties, like the ones we make. Right?

That's a pretty SAGE observation . . .

Céline's Granola

I remember occasionally coming home from school and being surprised to find a whole tray of granola sitting on the stove, still warm. My brother and I would scoop up as much granola as would fit in our little hands for the best snack. I'm not even joking—my mom (Céline!) would make so much granola that our cupboard would be filled with deli containers of it. The almonds, coconut, and maple syrup give this granola a sweet and nutty flavor that will always remind me of my childhood. To customize your granola, you can add ¼ cup of raw pepitas (pumpkin seeds), raw peanuts, walnuts, or shelled pistachios in step 2 or stir in ¼ cup of dried cherries after the granola cools in step 4.

MAKES about 5 cups
TOTAL TIME 1¼ hours, plus cooling time

Prepare Ingredients

- 3 cups (9 ounces) gluten-free old-fashioned rolled oats
- 1 cup (2½ ounces) unsweetened coconut chips
- 1 cup sliced almonds
- ½ cup maple syrup
- ½ cup refined coconut oil, melted and cooled but still liquid (see page 16)
- 1 teaspoon kosher salt
- 1 teaspoon ground cinnamon
- 1 teaspoon ground cardamom

Gather Cooking Equipment

- ▷ Large bowl
- ▷ Rubber spatula
- ▷ Rimmed baking sheet
- ▷ Oven mitts
- ▷ Cooling rack

Start Cooking!

1. Adjust oven rack to middle position and heat oven to 300 degrees.

2. In large bowl, use rubber spatula to stir all ingredients until well combined. Transfer oat mixture to rimmed baking sheet and spread into even layer.

3. Place baking sheet in oven. Bake until golden brown, 45 minutes to 1 hour, stirring every 15 minutes (ask an adult for help).

4. Use oven mitts to remove baking sheet from oven and place on cooling rack (ask an adult for help). Let granola cool completely, about 30 minutes. Serve. (Granola can be stored in airtight container for up to 2 weeks.)

How to Eat Granola

You can eat this granola in a bowl with yogurt or milk, maybe with some fresh fruit. Or you can eat it like Verveine and I do . . .

. . . right out of the jar—kind of like breakfast popcorn!

Usually only about half the recipe actually makes it into the storage container. We eat the rest right off the baking sheet. It's got just the right amount of salt that makes you want to go back for handful after handful.

Chapter 2

Pasta, Noodles, and Rice

intermediate

Spaghetti Carbonara

Spaghetti Carbonara has been on the menu at Coppa, one of my dad's restaurants, since the day it opened, which means I've been basically eating this dish since I was a baby. It's cheesy. It's egg yolky. It's super delicious. One day, not long after I learned how to read, we were eating at Coppa and I realized the menu said that my dad's version of carbonara had sea urchin in it. Sea urchin! I had no idea. We didn't put sea urchin in THIS recipe, but I will say that it's one of my favorite things and I recommend you try it (see page 173)! We love a combination of Parmesan and Pecorino Romano cheeses in this recipe, but you can use 1 cup of Parmesan, if you like. For information on our favorite gluten-free pasta, see page 12.

4 ⊞ **SERVES** 4
    TOTAL TIME 45 minutes

Prepare Ingredients

4   ounces bacon or pancetta, cut
    into ¼-inch pieces

5   large egg yolks (see page 16)

½   cup grated Parmesan cheese
    (1 ounce), plus extra for serving

½   cup grated Pecorino Romano
    cheese (1 ounce)

¼   teaspoon pepper

4   quarts water

2   tablespoons kosher salt

12 ounces gluten-free spaghetti

Gather Cooking Equipment

▷   10-inch skillet

▷   Slotted spoon

▷   Large heatproof bowl

▷   Rubber spatula

▷   Colander

▷   Large pot

▷   Wooden spoon

▷   Ladle

▷   Liquid measuring cup

▷   Whisk

▷   Tongs

Start Cooking!

1. In 10-inch skillet, cook bacon over medium heat until browned and crispy, 5 to 10 minutes. Turn off heat. Use slotted spoon to transfer bacon to large heatproof bowl.

2. Add egg yolks, Parmesan, Pecorino, and pepper to bowl with bacon. Use rubber spatula to stir until well combined and mixture looks like paste.

3. Set colander in sink. Add water to large pot. Bring to a boil over high heat. Carefully add salt and then pasta to pot. Cook, stirring often with wooden spoon, until pasta is al dente (tender but still a bit chewy), 10 to 12 minutes. Turn off heat.

4. Use ladle to carefully transfer ¾ cup pasta cooking water to liquid measuring cup. Ask an adult to drain pasta in colander in sink.

5. Whisk ⅓ cup reserved cooking water into egg mixture until well combined (see photo, below). Add pasta and use tongs to toss until pasta is well coated in creamy sauce.

6. If sauce is too thick, add remaining cooking water, a little bit at a time, and toss to combine. Season with salt and pepper to taste (see page 15). Serve with extra Parmesan.

How to Make Creamy Carbonara

Slowly whisk ⅓ cup pasta cooking water into egg mixture until well combined. (If you don't add the hot pasta cooking water slowly, you'll end up with scrambled eggs!)

beginner

Pasta with Pepita Pesto

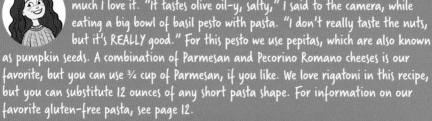

When I was 7 years old, I made a YouTube video all about pesto and how much I love it. "It tastes olive oil-y, salty," I said to the camera, while eating a big bowl of basil pesto with pasta. "I don't really taste the nuts, but it's REALLY good." For this pesto we use pepitas, which are also known as pumpkin seeds. A combination of Parmesan and Pecorino Romano cheeses is our favorite, but you can use ¾ cup of Parmesan, if you like. We love rigatoni in this recipe, but you can substitute 12 ounces of any short pasta shape. For information on our favorite gluten-free pasta, see page 12.

Prepare Ingredients

2½	cups fresh basil leaves
½	cup baby spinach
⅓	cup pepitas
1	small garlic clove, smashed and peeled (see page 17)
⅓	cup extra-virgin olive oil
½	cup grated Parmesan cheese (1 ounce)
¼	cup grated Pecorino Romano cheese (½ ounce)
4	quarts water
2	tablespoons kosher salt
12	ounces gluten-free rigatoni pasta

Gather Cooking Equipment

▷ Food processor
▷ Rubber spatula
▷ Large bowl
▷ Large pot
▷ Wooden spoon
▷ Spider skimmer or colander

Start Cooking!

1. Add basil, spinach, pepitas, and garlic to food processor. Lock lid into place. Turn on processor and process until mixture forms coarse puree, about 30 seconds. With processor running, drizzle in oil through feed tube and process until smooth, about 15 seconds.

2. Stop processor and remove lid. Add Parmesan and Pecorino and lock lid back into place. Hold down pulse button for 1 second, then release. Repeat pulsing until combined, about five 1-second pulses. Remove lid and carefully remove processor blade (ask an adult for help).

3. Use rubber spatula to transfer pesto to large bowl.

4. Add water to large pot. Bring to a boil over high heat. Carefully add salt and then pasta to pot. Cook, stirring often with wooden spoon, until pasta is al dente (tender but still a bit chewy), 10 to 12 minutes. Turn off heat.

5. Use spider skimmer to transfer pasta to large bowl with pesto (if you don't have a spider skimmer, ask an adult to drain the pasta in a colander in the sink).

6. Toss until well combined and pasta is coated in pesto. Season with salt and pepper to taste (see page 15). Serve.

A Twist on Tradition

In Italy, pesto is traditionally made with basil and pine nuts. Our recipe uses pepitas instead.

 Why did you switch from pine nuts to pepitas?

 They're delicious. They're nutritious. And it's easier for school lunch and allergen requirements, since pepitas are seeds, not nuts.

 Does it taste different?

 I actually like it better—it tastes more balanced.

advanced

Coppa Bolognese

I've been eating pasta with Bolognese forever and the version from my dad's restaurant, Coppa, is my favorite. Eating it brings back happy memories of sitting on our kitchen countertop and helping my dad cook. So what are you waiting for? Go ahead and make some memories! We like to use three meats in our Bolognese—beef, pork, and turkey—but you can use just one or two, if you like. This recipe makes a big batch of sauce, so be sure to freeze the extra for later. You can use 1 cup of chicken broth instead of the white wine, if you prefer. We love tagliatelle with our Bolognese, but you can use 12 ounces of any long, flat pasta shape. For information on our favorite gluten-free pasta, see page 12.

4 ⊞ **SERVES** 4 (Makes 12 cups sauce, enough for six 12-ounce batches of pasta)
TOTAL TIME 3 hours

Prepare Ingredients

BOLOGNESE

- 2 onions, peeled and chopped (see page 17)
- 2 carrots, peeled and chopped
- 4 celery ribs, chopped
- 3 garlic cloves, peeled and chopped (see page 17)
- ¼ cup extra-virgin olive oil
- 2 bay leaves
- ½ teaspoon pepper
- 1 teaspoon kosher salt
- 1 pound 85 percent lean ground beef
- 1 pound ground pork
- 1 pound ground turkey
- 1 cup white wine (see note, below left)
- 2 cups whole milk
- 2 (28-ounce) cans crushed tomatoes
- 1 cup chicken broth
- 1 tablespoon tamari
- 3 tablespoons unsalted butter, cut into 6 pieces
- ⅛ teaspoon ground nutmeg

FOR 4 SERVINGS

- 4 quarts water
- 2 tablespoons kosher salt
- 12 ounces gluten-free tagliatelle pasta
- 2 cups Bolognese
  Grated Parmesan cheese

Gather Cooking Equipment

- ▷ Food processor
- ▷ Rubber spatula
- ▷ Dutch oven
- ▷ Wooden spoon
- ▷ Colander
- ▷ Large pot
- ▷ Ladle
- ▷ Liquid measuring cup
- ▷ 11-inch sauté pan or 12-inch skillet
- ▷ Tongs

Start Cooking!

1. FOR THE BOLOGNESE: Add onions, carrots, celery, and garlic to food processor. Lock lid into place. Turn on processor and process for 30 seconds. Stop processor and remove lid. Use rubber spatula to scrape down sides of processor bowl. Lock lid back into place. Turn on processor and process until vegetables form puree and liquid is released, about 30 seconds. Stop processor. Remove lid and carefully remove processor blade (ask an adult for help).

2. In Dutch oven, combine pureed vegetables, oil, bay leaves, pepper, and 1 teaspoon salt. Cook over medium heat, stirring occasionally with wooden spoon, until vegetables soften, about 20 minutes.

3. Add ground beef, pork, and turkey to pot. Use wooden spoon to stir and break up meat into small pieces. Add wine and cook, continuing to stir to break up meat, until meat is no longer pink, about 10 minutes.

4. Add milk and increase heat to medium-high. Bring to rapid simmer (small bubbles should break constantly across surface of mixture) and cook until milk has reduced, about 15 minutes.

Keep Going!

5. Stir in tomatoes, chicken broth, and tamari and bring to simmer. Reduce heat to medium-low, and simmer, stirring occasionally, until liquid has reduced and sauce is thickened, about 1½ hours.

6. Stir in butter and nutmeg until well combined. Turn off heat. Remove and discard bay leaves. Season with salt and pepper to taste (see page 15).

7. FOR 4 SERVINGS: Place colander in sink. Add water to large pot. Bring to a boil over high heat. Carefully add 2 tablespoons salt and then pasta to pot. Cook, stirring often with clean wooden spoon, until pasta is al dente (tender but still a bit chewy), 10 to 12 minutes. Turn off heat.

8. Use ladle to carefully transfer ½ cup pasta cooking water to liquid measuring cup. Ask an adult to drain pasta in colander in sink. Transfer pasta to 11-inch sauté pan.

9. Add 2 cups Bolognese and reserved cooking water to pan with pasta. Cook over medium heat, tossing with tongs, until sauce thickens slightly and pasta is well coated in sauce, about 2 minutes. Turn off heat. Season with salt and pepper to taste (see page 15).

10. Serve with Parmesan. (Remaining Bolognese can be refrigerated for up to 4 days or frozen in 2-cup portions for up to 6 months.)

Verveine suddenly remembers that her dad adds some pasta water to the sauce for his Coppa Bolognese.

Pasta with Chicken and Broccoli Sugo

My dad originally created this dish for my brother and I when we were little to get us to eat broccoli without knowing it. It definitely worked! It's still one of my absolute favorite foods and, honestly, I didn't know there was broccoli in it until I started cooking it myself. I'll warn you: This is a project, but it's so worth it! This recipe makes a big batch of sauce, so freeze the extra for later. You can use ½ cup of chicken broth instead of the white wine, if you prefer. We love medium shells in this recipe, but you can use any short pasta shape. For information on our favorite gluten-free pasta, see page 12.

SERVES 4 (Makes 9 cups sauce, enough for three 12-ounce batches of pasta)
TOTAL TIME 2¼ hours, plus 1 hour chilling time

Prepare Ingredients

SAUSAGE

2	pounds ground chicken or turkey
3	garlic cloves, peeled and chopped (see page 17)
1	tablespoon smoked paprika
1	tablespoon kosher salt
2	teaspoons ground fennel
2	teaspoons ground coriander
½	teaspoon red pepper flakes
½	teaspoon pepper

SAUCE

1	pound broccoli crowns, roughly chopped
3	tablespoons extra-virgin olive oil
1	onion, peeled and finely chopped (see page 17)
1	garlic clove, peeled
½	cup white wine (see note, below left)
2	cups chicken broth
2	(28-ounce) cans crushed tomatoes
1	bay leaf

FOR 4 SERVINGS

4	quarts water
2	tablespoons kosher salt
12	ounces gluten-free medium shells
3	cups Chicken and Broccoli Sugo
	Grated Parmesan cheese

Gather Cooking Equipment

▷ 2 large bowls
▷ Rubber spatula
▷ Plastic wrap
▷ Rimmed baking sheet
▷ Oven mitts
▷ Cooling rack
▷ Food processor
▷ Dutch oven
▷ Wooden spoon
▷ Large pot
▷ 11-inch sauté pan or 12-inch skillet
▷ Ladle
▷ Liquid measuring cup
▷ Spider skimmer or colander

From Chef Ken: What is Sugo?

"Sugo" means "sauce" or "juice" in Italian—it can refer to fruit juice, the juices in cooked meat, or a sauce for pasta like this one. This particular sugo is definitely a big project: First you make the sausage, and then you need to prep and simmer the sugo, all before tossing it with your pasta. That's why it's worth taking the time to make a really big batch. This way you can freeze some for quick and easy future dinners (or lunches or breakfasts—there's never a bad time for sugo).

Keep Going!

Start Cooking!

1. FOR THE SAUSAGE: In large bowl, combine all sausage ingredients. Use rubber spatula to stir until well combined. Cover bowl with plastic wrap and refrigerate for at least 1 hour or up to 24 hours.

2. Adjust oven rack to middle position and heat oven to 325 degrees. Spread ground chicken mixture over rimmed baking sheet. Place baking sheet in oven. Bake until sausage is cooked through and lightly browned, 15 to 18 minutes.

3. Use oven mitts to remove baking sheet from oven and place on cooling rack (ask an adult for help). Let sausage cool completely, about 15 minutes.

4. FOR THE SAUCE: Add broccoli to food processor. Lock lid into place. Hold down pulse button for 1 second, then release. Repeat until broccoli is finely ground, twenty to twenty-five 1-second pulses. Remove lid and carefully remove processor blade (ask an adult for help). Use clean rubber spatula to transfer broccoli to second large bowl.

5. Carefully replace processor blade (ask an adult for help). Add cooled sausage to now-empty food processor. Lock lid back into place. Pulse until sausage is finely ground, ten to twelve 1-second pulses. Transfer to bowl with broccoli.

6. In Dutch oven, combine oil, onion, and garlic. Cook over medium heat, stirring occasionally with wooden spoon, until softened, about 7 minutes.

7. Add sausage and broccoli and cook, stirring occasionally, until broccoli loses its vibrant color, about 8 minutes.

8. Stir in wine and cook until no liquid remains, 2 to 4 minutes. Add chicken broth, tomatoes, and bay leaf and bring to simmer (small bubbles should break often across surface of sauce). Reduce heat to low, and cook until chunky and thickened, 35 to 45 minutes. Turn off heat. Remove and discard bay leaf. Season with salt and pepper to taste (see page 15).

9. FOR 4 SERVINGS: Add water to large pot. Bring to a boil over high heat. Carefully add 2 tablespoons salt and then pasta to pot. Cook, stirring often with clean wooden spoon, until pasta is al dente (tender but still a bit chewy), 10 to 12 minutes. Turn off heat.

10. Add 3 cups chicken and broccoli sugo to 11-inch sauté pan. Use ladle to carefully transfer ¼ cup pasta cooking water to liquid measuring cup. Use spider skimmer to transfer pasta to pan with sauce (if you don't have a spider skimmer, ask an adult to drain the pasta in a colander in the sink).

11. Add reserved cooking water to pan with pasta. Cook over medium heat, stirring occasionally, until until pasta is well coated with sauce, about 2 minutes. Turn off heat.

12. Serve with Parmesan cheese. (Remaining sauce can be refrigerated for up to 4 days or frozen in 3-cup portions for up to 6 months.)

Spicy Sicilian Tuna Pasta

When I was 9 years old, I traveled to Europe with my family, where I was officially introduced to canned tuna in oil. I had never tried tuna that tasted like THIS before. It was packed in oil and tasted so satisfying and full of umami (see page 14). When we got home, we ate the tuna with tortilla chips, but eventually we came up with our own version of Sicilian tuna pasta using canned tuna and tomato sauce. This immediately became a favorite in our house—it's a great recipe for quick dinners, having people over, and delicious lunches. We love garganelli in this recipe, but you can use 12 ounces of any short pasta shape. For information on our favorite gluten-free pasta, see page 12.

Prepare Ingredients

- 1 tablespoon extra-virgin olive oil
- 1 garlic clove, peeled and minced (see page 17)
- ⅛ teaspoon dried oregano
- ⅛–¼ teaspoon red pepper flakes
- 1 (6-ounce) can solid white tuna in olive oil
- 1 (14.5-ounce) can crushed tomatoes
- ⅛ teaspoon fish sauce
- 4 quarts water
- 2 tablespoons kosher salt
- 12 ounces gluten-free garganelli pasta
- Chopped fresh mint (see page 17) (optional)

Gather Cooking Equipment

- ▷ 11-inch sauté pan or 12-inch skillet
- ▷ Wooden spoon
- ▷ Large pot
- ▷ Ladle
- ▷ Liquid measuring cup
- ▷ Spider skimmer or colander

Start Cooking!

1. In 11-inch sauté pan combine oil, garlic, oregano, and red pepper flakes. Cook over medium heat until fragrant, about 1 minute.

2. Add tuna and oil from can to pan. Use wooden spoon to flake tuna into small pieces. Add tomatoes and fish sauce and stir to combine. Bring to simmer (small bubbles should break often across surface of sauce), and cook until sauce thickens slightly, about 5 minutes. Turn off heat.

3. Add water to large pot. Bring to a boil over high heat. Carefully add salt and then pasta to pot. Cook, stirring often with clean wooden spoon, until pasta is al dente (tender but still a bit chewy), 10 to 12 minutes. Turn off heat.

4. Use ladle to carefully transfer ¼ cup pasta cooking water to liquid measuring cup. Use spider skimmer to transfer pasta to sauté pan with sauce (if you don't have a spider skimmer, ask an adult to drain the pasta in a colander in the sink).

5. Add reserved cooking water to pan with pasta and sauce. Cook over medium heat, stirring occasionally, until pasta is well coated with sauce, about 2 minutes. Turn off heat. Season with salt and pepper to taste (see page 15). Serve, sprinkling individual portions with mint (if using).

From Chef Ken: Next-Level Tuna

This pasta is traditionally made in Sicily, the island just off the "toe" of Italy's "boot." Sicilians, despite being surrounded by water, love to cook with canned or jarred tuna packed in oil. It's moist, tender, silky, and savory— much more so than canned tuna that's packed in water. I like to pack as much umami (savory taste) into my dishes as possible (see page 14), so in addition to the tuna I add a little fish sauce to this recipe. Fish sauce is full of umami (see "An Ode to Fish Sauce," page 93) and will not make this sauce taste fishy, I promise.

intermediate

Spaghetti al Limone

The first time my dad made this dish for our family, I have to admit that it was WAY too lemony. But we worked on it together, and I'm proud to say that it's now the perfect dish for a hot summer night. It's so fresh, and it's nice to slurp the spaghetti! I recommend you serve this as part of an all-lemon dinner with Céline's Lemon Squares (page 186) for dessert. For information on our favorite gluten-free pasta, see page 12.

Prepare Ingredients

½ cup gluten-free bread crumbs

1 tablespoon plus 2 tablespoons extra-virgin olive oil, measured separately

1 garlic clove, peeled and chopped (see page 17)

4 quarts water

2 tablespoons kosher salt

12 ounces gluten-free spaghetti

2 tablespoons unsalted butter, cut into 4 pieces and chilled

1 cup grated Parmesan cheese (2 ounces), plus extra for serving

1 tablespoon grated lemon zest plus ⅓ cup lemon juice, zested and squeezed from 2 lemons

Gather Cooking Equipment

▷ 10-inch skillet

▷ Wooden spoon

▷ Small bowl

▷ 11-inch sauté pan or 12-inch skillet

▷ Colander

▷ Large pot

▷ Ladle

▷ Liquid measuring cup

▷ Tongs

Start Cooking!

1. In 10-inch skillet, combine bread crumbs and 1 tablespoon oil. Cook over medium-low heat, stirring occasionally with wooden spoon, until bread crumbs turn light golden, 3 to 5 minutes. Turn off heat. Transfer bread crumbs to small bowl.

2. In 11-inch sauté pan, combine garlic and remaining 2 tablespoons oil. Cook over medium heat, stirring often, until fragrant, about 1 minute. Turn off heat and slide pan to cool burner.

3. Place colander in sink. Add water to large pot. Bring to a boil over high heat. Carefully add salt and then pasta to pot. Cook, stirring often with clean wooden spoon, until pasta is al dente (tender but still a bit chewy), 10 to 12 minutes. Turn off heat.

4. Use ladle to carefully transfer ½ cup pasta cooking water to liquid measuring cup. Ask an adult to drain pasta in colander in sink.

5. Add cold butter and reserved cooking water to pan with garlic, and cook over medium heat, swirling pan to emulsify sauce, about 2 minutes (see "All About Emulsions," below). Transfer pasta to sauté pan with sauce. Use tongs to toss pasta until well combined. Add Parmesan and toss to combine. Add lemon juice and continue to toss until pasta is well coated in sauce. Turn off heat.

6. Season with salt and pepper to taste (see page 15). Serve, sprinkling individual portions with lemon zest, toasted bread crumbs, and extra Parmesan.

From Chef Ken: All About Emulsions

An emulsion is a smooth mixture of two liquids that wouldn't ordinarily combine, like oil and water. While the emulsion that first comes to mind might be vinaigrette dressing (vinegar is mostly water), this pasta sauce is an emulsion, too. It contains olive oil and lemon juice (also mostly water). If you pour oil and water into a container, they'll form two separate layers. But there are a few tricks to keep an emulsion combined. You can whisk or shake it up, like in a salad dressing. You can also add another ingredient to the mix, called an emulsifier. Our emulsifier: pasta cooking water. Its starch helps bridge the gap between the oil and the lemon juice, making our sauce creamy and smooth.

Fresh Pasta

I would argue that this is one of the most important recipes in the entire book—or at least in this chapter! This gluten-free fresh pasta is a staple for my dad and me. It can be made into any shape and served with any sauce. The best part is that no one can tell it's gluten free! We strongly prefer Cup4Cup Gluten-Free Multipurpose Flour in this recipe—if you use King Arthur Gluten-Free Measure for Measure Flour, the dough will be drier and harder to work with. For more information on gluten-free flours, see page 12. This pasta is great with just butter and Parmesan cheese, but I also love it with any of the sauces in this chapter.

SERVES 4
TOTAL TIME 45 minutes, plus 30 minutes resting time

Prepare Ingredients

PASTA

2 cups (10 ounces) Cup4Cup Gluten-Free Multipurpose Flour, plus extra for shaping

2¼ teaspoons kosher salt

1 large egg plus 7 large egg yolks (see page 16)

2 tablespoons water

TO FINISH

4 quarts water

2 tablespoons kosher salt

4 tablespoons unsalted butter, cut into 4 pieces

½ cup grated Parmesan cheese (1 ounce)

Gather Cooking Equipment

▷ Fork

▷ Plastic wrap

▷ Bench scraper or chef's knife

▷ Rolling pin

▷ Ruler

▷ Electric or manual pasta machine

▷ Rimmed baking sheet

▷ Parchment paper

▷ Colander

▷ Large pot

▷ Wooden spoon

▷ Large serving bowl

▷ Tongs

Start Cooking!

1. FOR THE PASTA: On clean counter, use your fingers to combine flour and 2¼ teaspoons salt. Make well in center of flour and add whole egg, egg yolks, and 2 tablespoons water. Slowly stir with fork until dough comes together.

2. Use your hands to knead dough until smooth ball forms and no dry flour remains, about 3 minutes.

3. Wrap pasta dough in plastic wrap. Place dough in refrigerator and let rest for at least 30 minutes or up to 24 hours.

4. Lightly dust clean counter with extra flour. Use bench scraper to divide dough into 6 equal pieces and cover with plastic. Working with 1 piece of dough at a time, roll and cut pasta following photos, pages 72–73. (Pasta nests can be refrigerated in an airtight container for up to 2 days.)

5. TO FINISH: Place colander in sink. Add 4 quarts water to large pot. Bring to a boil over high heat. Carefully add 2 tablespoons salt and then pasta to pot. Cook, stirring often with wooden spoon, until pasta is al dente (tender but still a bit chewy), 5 to 7 minutes. Turn off heat.

6. Add butter to large serving bowl. Ask an adult to drain pasta in colander in sink. Transfer pasta to bowl. Use tongs to toss until butter melts. Add Parmesan and toss until pasta is well coated with butter and cheese. Season with salt and pepper to taste (see page 15). Serve.

Keep Going!

The Pasta Maker's Journey

We've eaten a lot of gluten-free pasta.

Yeah, I've been working on gluten-free fresh pasta for a long time.

You've had your ups and downs. I'd come home from school and there would be so many flours on the counter!

Ha, yes. I spent a lot of time experimenting: weighing things by the gram, making it perfect.

How to Make Fresh Pasta

It is much easier to roll the dough out by hand a little bit before feeding it through the pasta machine. If the pasta is too thick when you add it to the machine, it will turn into a hot mess!

1. Working with 1 piece of dough at a time, use rolling pin to roll dough into long rectangle-ish shape, about 7 inches long and 3½ inches wide (this rectangular shape is important!). Make sure pasta is a little smaller than width of rollers.

2. Set pasta machine rollers to widest, most open position (usually the lowest number setting). Guide and feed dough through machine. Feed dough through machine a second time.

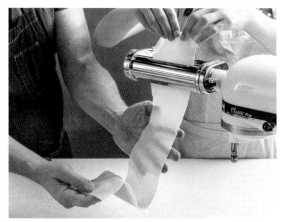

3. Lightly dust dough with flour and fold dough in half. Narrow rollers by one number. Feed dough through machine. Lightly dust dough with flour, fold dough in half, and narrow rollers again by one number. Feed dough through machine again.

4. Repeat dusting with flour, folding, and feeding dough through machine (narrowing roller by one number each time) until you can see your hand through dough.

5. Place dough on lightly floured counter and use bench scraper to cut in half crosswise (the short way). Repeat rolling and cutting remaining pieces of dough.

6. Change attachment on pasta machine to fettuccine or tagliatelle attachment. Line rimmed baking sheet with parchment paper and lightly dust with flour. Feed 1 pasta sheet through rollers to cut into strands. Use your hands to gently twirl pasta strands into nest on baking sheet. Repeat cutting and twirling with remaining sheets of dough.

advanced

Spinach Orecchiette

Orecchiette is my favorite pasta shape. Each one looks like a beautiful smushed ball (or a "little ear," the Italian translation of the name!). This version is a vibrant shade of green, but it doesn't taste green, I promise. When you pull the pasta out of the water, it looks like the Loch Ness Monster. This spinach orecchiette is great with butter and Parmesan cheese, but you can also serve it with any of the sauces in this chapter. For information on substituting gluten-free flours, see page 12.

Prepare Ingredients

ORECCHIETTE

- 2 cups (2 ounces) baby spinach
- 2 large eggs
- ¼ cup (2 ounces) milk
- 2 cups (10 ounces) Cup4Cup Gluten-Free Multipurpose Flour, plus extra for shaping
- ¼ teaspoon kosher salt

TO FINISH

- 4 quarts water
- 2 tablespoons kosher salt
- 4 tablespoons unsalted butter, cut into 4 pieces
- ½ cup grated Parmesan cheese (1 ounce)

Gather Cooking Equipment

- ▷ Blender
- ▷ Dish towel
- ▷ Large bowl
- ▷ Fork
- ▷ Plastic wrap
- ▷ Rimmed baking sheet
- ▷ Parchment paper
- ▷ Bench scraper or butter knife
- ▷ Ruler
- ▷ Large pot
- ▷ Wooden spoon
- ▷ Large serving bowl
- ▷ Spider skimmer or colander

Start Cooking!

1. FOR THE ORECCHIETTE: Add spinach, eggs, and milk to blender jar. Place lid on top of blender and hold lid firmly in place with folded dish towel. Turn on blender and process until smooth, about 1 minute. Stop blender.

2. In large bowl, add flour and sprinkle with ¼ teaspoon salt. Use your hands to make well in center of flour. Pour spinach mixture into well in bowl. Use fork to slowly stir to bring flour and spinach mixture together until dough starts to form.

3. Sprinkle clean counter with extra flour and transfer dough to counter. Use your hands to knead dough until smooth, about 1 minute, adding a little extra flour if dough feels too sticky. Form dough into smooth ball. Wrap dough in plastic wrap. Place in refrigerator and let rest for at least 30 minutes or up to 2 days.

4. Line rimmed baking sheet with parchment paper and sprinkle lightly with extra flour. Cut, roll, and shape orecchiette following photos, page 76. (Orecchiette can be refrigerated in an airtight container for up to 24 hours.)

5. TO FINISH: Add water to large pot. Bring to a boil over high heat. Carefully add 2 tablespoons salt and then orecchiette to pot. Cook, stirring often with wooden spoon, until pasta is al dente (tender but still a bit chewy), 5 to 7 minutes. Turn off heat.

6. Add butter to large serving bowl. Use spider skimmer to transfer pasta to serving bowl (if you don't have a spider skimmer, ask an adult to drain the pasta in a colander in the sink).

7. Use wooden spoon to toss until butter melts. Add Parmesan and stir gently until pasta is well coated with butter and cheese. Season to taste with salt and pepper (see page 15). Serve.

Keep Going!

How to Shape Orecchiette

1. Lightly sprinkle extra flour on counter and sprinkle dough with flour. Use bench scraper to divide dough into 6 equal pieces.

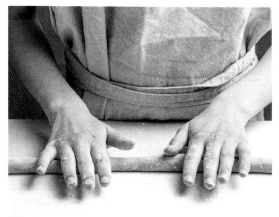

2. Working with 1 piece of dough at a time (keeping remaining dough covered in plastic), roll dough into ½-inch thick rope, about 16 inches long.

3. Dip bench scraper in extra flour. Cut dough crosswise (the short way) into ¼-inch pieces.

4. Dust your fingers with extra flour. Turn each piece cut side up and press your thumb into the dough to make it look like an ear. Use bench scraper to carefully transfer orecchiette to parchment-lined rimmed baking sheet dusted with flour. Repeat rolling, cutting, and shaping with remaining 5 pieces of dough.

Pasta al Forno with Five Cheeses

I am very particular about my baked pastas. I love a crispy top and a creamy interior. But it can't be TOO crispy, and it can't be TOO creamy. This dish fits my exacting criteria—it's cheesy but not TOO cheesy! It's great comfort food for a cold winter night. We love penne in this recipe, but you can substitute 12 ounces of any short pasta shape. For information on our favorite gluten-free pasta, see page 12.

SERVES 4
TOTAL TIME 1 hour

Prepare Ingredients

1¾ cups heavy cream

1¼ cups (10 ounces) canned crushed tomatoes

1 cup shredded mozzarella cheese (4 ounces)

½ cup grated Parmesan cheese (1 ounce)

½ cup shredded fontina cheese (2 ounces)

2 tablespoons crumbled gorgonzola cheese

2 tablespoons whole-milk ricotta cheese

1 teaspoon plus 2 tablespoons kosher salt, measured separately

4 quarts water

12 ounces gluten-free penne pasta

4 tablespoons unsalted butter, cut into 8 pieces

Gather Cooking Equipment

▷ Large bowl
▷ Rubber spatula
▷ Large pot
▷ Wooden spoon
▷ Spider skimmer or colander
▷ 13-by-9-inch baking dish
▷ Oven mitts
▷ Cooling rack

Start Cooking!

1. Adjust oven rack to middle position and heat oven to 500 degrees.

2. In large bowl, combine heavy cream, tomatoes, all five cheeses, and 1 teaspoon salt. Use rubber spatula to stir until well combined.

3. Add water to large pot. Bring to a boil over high heat. Carefully add remaining 2 tablespoons salt and then pasta to pot. Cook, stirring often with wooden spoon, until pasta is just starting to soften, 6 to 8 minutes (it will finish cooking in the oven). Turn off heat.

4. Use spider skimmer to transfer pasta to bowl with cheese mixture (if you don't have a spider skimmer, ask an adult to drain the pasta in a colander in the sink). Stir until pasta is well coated with sauce.

5. Pour pasta mixture into 13-by-9-inch baking dish. Scatter butter pieces over top.

6. Place baking dish in oven. Bake until bubbling and cheese is browned and crispy on top, 12 to 15 minutes.

7. Use oven mitts to remove baking dish from oven and place on cooling rack (ask an adult for help). Let cool for 10 minutes. Serve.

A TALE OF FIVE CHEESES

Each of the cheeses in this recipe brings something special to this pasta party.

GORGONZOLA
Extra umami kick—a little goes a long way!

RICOTTA
Rich, creamy texture

PARMESAN
Salty and savory—there's no better cheese in the world!

MOZZARELLA
Even more melty goodness

FONTINA
Melty and stringy, but not TOO stringy

advanced

Potato Gnocchi

My favorite thing about gnocchi is how light, fluffy, and pillowy they are. Ever since we were little, my brother Luca and I have loved smushing these little potato pillows under our tongues. They melt right in your mouth! These gnocchi are delicious with just butter and Parmesan, but I absolutely love them with Vodka Sauce (page 84). For information on substituting gluten-free flours, see page 12.

SERVES 4 to 6
TOTAL TIME 2½ hours

Prepare Ingredients

GNOCCHI

2 pounds russet potatoes

1 cup (5 ounces) Cup4Cup Gluten-Free Multipurpose Flour, plus extra for shaping

⅛ teaspoon pepper

½ teaspoon kosher salt

2 large eggs

TO FINISH

4 quarts water

2 tablespoons kosher salt

4 tablespoons unsalted butter, cut into 4 pieces

½ cup grated Parmesan cheese (1 ounce)

Gather Cooking Equipment

▷ Fork

▷ 2 rimmed baking sheets

▷ Oven mitts

▷ Cooling rack

▷ Paring knife

▷ Potato ricer or food mill

▷ Bench scraper or chef's knife

▷ Ruler

▷ Large pot

▷ Spider skimmer or slotted spoon

▷ Large serving bowl

▷ Rubber spatula

Start Cooking!

1. FOR THE GNOCCHI: Adjust oven rack to middle position and heat oven to 400 degrees. Wash potatoes and poke them all over with fork. Arrange potatoes on rimmed baking sheet. Place baking sheet in oven. Bake until very soft, about 1 hour.

2. Use oven mitts to remove baking sheet from oven and place on cooling rack (ask an adult for help). Ask an adult to cut slit down middle of each potato to let steam escape—potatoes will be very HOT!

3. Scoop or squeeze potato flesh out of skins into potato ricer. Pass potatoes through potato ricer onto clean counter. Let cool slightly, about 5 minutes.

4. Once potatoes are cool enough to handle, make a well in the center. Sprinkle flour, pepper, and ½ teaspoon salt over potatoes. Add eggs to well in potatoes. Use clean fork to stir and bring mixture together, and continue to stir until well combined. If dough is sticky, sprinkle with a little extra flour. Knead until dough forms that is neither sticky nor dry, about 1 minute.

5. Sprinkle second rimmed baking sheet with extra flour. Use bench scraper to cut dough into 8 equal pieces. Sprinkle counter and your hands lightly with flour. Working with 1 piece of dough at a time, shape gnocchi following photos, page 82. (Uncooked gnocchi can be refrigerated, uncovered, for up to 3 hours.)

6. TO FINISH: Add water to large pot. Bring to a boil over high heat. Carefully add 2 tablespoons salt and then half of gnocchi to pot. Use spider skimmer to stir once to make sure gnocchi do not stick to bottom of pot. Reduce heat to medium-high. Cook at low boil until gnocchi float to surface of water. Then continue to cook until tender, 3 to 5 minutes. (You want the water at a low boil, not a rapid boil while cooking gnocchi—adjust heat as needed.)

7. Add butter to large serving bowl. Use spider skimmer to transfer gnocchi to serving bowl. Repeat cooking with remaining gnocchi. Turn off heat.

8. Use rubber spatula to toss until butter melts. Add Parmesan and stir gently until gnocchi are well coated with butter and Parmesan. Serve.

Keep Going!

How to Shape Gnocchi

1. On lightly floured counter, roll 1 piece of dough into ¾-inch thick rope, about 20 inches long.

2. Use bench scraper to cut dough crosswise (the short way) into ¾-inch pieces.

3. Sprinkle a little more flour over top of gnocchi and carefully transfer to lightly floured rimmed baking sheet. Repeat rolling and cutting with remaining 7 pieces of dough.

From Chef Ken: Make-Ahead Gnocchi

Making gnocchi is a big project! You can make and cook your gnocchi ahead of time. Then, when you want to eat, all you have to do is reheat the precooked gnocchi right in your sauce. Here's how to do it.

While gnocchi cook in step 6, fill medium bowl with cold water. When gnocchi are done cooking, use spider skimmer to transfer gnocchi to bowl of cold water. Let sit for 1 minute. Drain gnocchi in colander in sink and transfer to large bowl. Toss with 2 tablespoons extra virgin olive oil. Repeat with remaining gnocchi. (Cooked gnocchi can be refrigerated for up to 2 days or frozen for up to 3 months.)

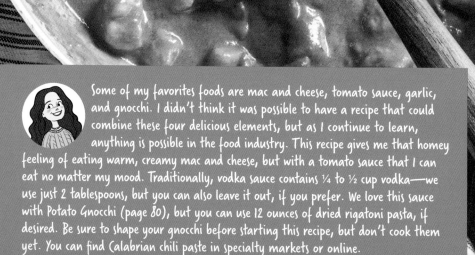

Vodka Sauce with Potato Gnocchi

Some of my favorites foods are mac and cheese, tomato sauce, garlic, and gnocchi. I didn't think it was possible to have a recipe that could combine these four delicious elements, but as I continue to learn, anything is possible in the food industry. This recipe gives me that homey feeling of eating warm, creamy mac and cheese, but with a tomato sauce that I can eat no matter my mood. Traditionally, vodka sauce contains ¼ to ½ cup vodka—we use just 2 tablespoons, but you can also leave it out, if you prefer. We love this sauce with Potato Gnocchi (page 80), but you can use 12 ounces of dried rigatoni pasta, if desired. Be sure to shape your gnocchi before starting this recipe, but don't cook them yet. You can find Calabrian chili paste in specialty markets or online.

Prepare Ingredients

1	recipe Potato Gnocchi (page 80), shaped but not cooked
1	tablespoon extra-virgin olive oil
3	garlic cloves, peeled and minced (see page 17)
½–1	teaspoon Calabrian chili paste or ⅛–¼ teaspoon red pepper flakes
2	tablespoons vodka (optional)
1	(14.5-ounce) can crushed tomatoes
⅔	cup heavy cream
1	tablespoon unsalted butter
4	quarts water
2	tablespoons kosher salt
⅔	cup grated Parmesan cheese (1¼ ounces), plus extra for serving

Gather Cooking Equipment

▷ 11-inch sauté pan or 12-inch skillet

▷ Wooden spoon

▷ Large pot

▷ Spider skimmer or slotted spoon

▷ Ladle

▷ Liquid measuring cup

Start Cooking!

1. In 11-inch sauté pan, combine oil, garlic, and Calabrian chili paste. Cook over medium heat until fragrant, about 1 minute.

2. Turn off heat. Add vodka (if using) and stir with wooden spoon to combine. Return pan to medium heat and cook until almost no vodka remains, about 1 minute.

3. Add tomatoes to pan and cook, stirring often with wooden spoon, until sauce thickens to almost the consistency of paste, 5 to 7 minutes.

4. Stir in cream and butter and cook until well combined and sauce has consistency of creamy tomato soup, 5 to 7 minutes. Turn off heat.

5. Add water to large pot. Bring to a boil over high heat. Carefully add salt and then half of gnocchi to pot. Use spider skimmer to stir once to make sure gnocchi do not stick to bottom of pot. Reduce heat to medium-high. Cook at low boil until gnocchi float to surface of water. Then continue to cook until tender, 3 to 5 minutes. (You want the water at a low boil, not a rapid boil while cooking gnocchi—adjust heat as needed.)

6. Use spider skimmer to carefully transfer gnocchi to pan with sauce. Repeat cooking with remaining gnocchi. Turn off heat.

7. Use ladle to carefully transfer ¾ cup gnocchi cooking water to liquid measuring cup. Add ½ cup reserved cooking water to sauté pan with gnocchi and sauce. Very carefully stir gnocchi until well coated in sauce and cook over medium heat to warm through, about 1 minute.

8. Stir in Parmesan. If sauce is too thick, add remaining gnocchi cooking water, a little bit at a time, to loosen. Turn off heat.

9. Season with salt and pepper to taste (see page 15). Serve with extra Parmesan.

"Late-Night" Ramen

My dad and I are big fans of late-night snacks. We'll eat an early dinner, and then we'll eat popcorn or chocolate or something else later on. But this ramen is my absolute favorite late-night snack—especially when watching a movie. The broth makes me feel all warm and cozy, which is how you want to feel late at night. Plus, you can add all your favorite toppings! This recipe makes a big batch of broth, so be sure to freeze the extra for later. For information on our favorite gluten-free ramen, see page 12.

SERVES 1 (Makes 12 cups broth, enough for 6 servings of ramen)
TOTAL TIME 3¾ hours for broth, 15 minutes for ramen

Prepare Ingredients

RAMEN BROTH

- 3 pounds chicken wings
- 2 quarts water
- 2 quarts chicken broth
- 2 onions, peeled and chopped (see page 17)
- 1 carrot, washed, trimmed, and cut into 2-inch chunks
- 5 garlic cloves, peeled (see page 17)
- 1 (1-inch) piece of ginger, sliced thin (see page 18)
- 2 dried guajillo or pasilla chiles
- ½ teaspoon black peppercorns
- ½ cup red or white miso
- ¼ cup gluten-free tamari
- 4 tablespoons unsalted butter, cut into 4 pieces

FOR 1 SERVING

- 2 cups ramen broth
- 2½ ounces gluten-free ramen noodles
- 1 scallion, end trimmed and scallion sliced thin
- 1½ teaspoons toasted sesame seeds
  Additional toppings (see below) (optional)

Gather Cooking Equipment

▷ Large stock pot
▷ Fine-mesh strainer
▷ Large bowl
▷ Whisk
▷ Ladle
▷ Small saucepan
▷ Wooden spoon
▷ Serving bowl

Start Cooking!

1. FOR THE RAMEN BROTH: In large stock pot, combine chicken wings, water, broth, onions, carrot, garlic, ginger, chiles, and peppercorns. Bring to a boil over high heat. Reduce heat to low and simmer for 3 hours (small bubbles should break often across surface of broth). Turn off heat.

2. Place fine-mesh strainer over large bowl. Ask an adult to strain broth. Discard solids in strainer.

3. Return broth to now-empty stock pot. Bring to simmer over high heat. Add miso, tamari, and butter. Whisk until well combined. Turn off heat. (Broth can be cooled completely and refrigerated for up to 5 days or frozen in 2-cup portions for up to 6 months.)

4. FOR 1 SERVING: Ladle 2 cups ramen broth into small saucepan. Bring to a boil over medium-high heat. Carefully add ramen noodles and cook, stirring often with wooden spoon, until just tender, 3 to 4 minutes. Turn off heat.

5. Carefully pour ramen and broth into serving bowl. Sprinkle with scallion and sesame seeds, and add additional toppings (if using). Serve.

OUR FAVORITE RAMEN TOPPINGS

Sliced Cooked Hot Dogs

Chili-Garlic Sauce

Bean Sprouts

Nori Sheets

Shredded Chicken

Ramen Cacio e Pepe

My grandpa and I have three main things in common: We both love swimming, garlic, and black pepper. I have so many memories of making cacio e pepe at his house—it's a dish of cheesy pasta with LOTS of black pepper. One day, my dad thought it would be interesting to make cacio e pepe with chewy ramen noodles instead of pasta, and this amazing recipe was born. (Of course he also upped the umami by adding miso—see page 14). Make sure to use imported Pecorino Romano cheese made from sheep's milk. It's saltier, tangier, and more flavorful than domestic Romano cheese made from cow's milk. For information on our favorite gluten-free ramen, see page 12.

SERVES 4
TOTAL TIME 40 minutes

Prepare Ingredients

3 tablespoon extra-virgin olive oil

1 tablespoon pepper

2 tablespoons white or red miso paste

4 quarts water

12 ounces gluten-free ramen noodles

2 tablespoons unsalted butter, cut into 4 pieces and chilled

2 cups grated Pecorino Romano cheese (4 ounces), plus extra for serving

Gather Cooking Equipment

▷ 11-inch sauté pan or 12-inch skillet

▷ Wooden spoon

▷ Colander

▷ Large pot

▷ Ladle

▷ 2-cup liquid measuring cup

▷ Whisk

▷ Tongs

Start Cooking!

1. In 11-inch sauté pan, combine oil and pepper. Cook over medium heat until fragrant, about 1 minute. Add miso and use wooden spoon to stir until well combined. Turn off heat.

2. Place colander in sink. Add water to large pot. Bring to a boil over high heat. Carefully add ramen noodles to pot. Cook, stirring often with clean wooden spoon, until noodles are tender, 3 to 4 minutes. Turn off heat.

3. Use ladle to carefully transfer 1½ cups ramen cooking water to 2-cup liquid measuring cup. Ask an adult to drain noodles in colander in sink.

4. Add 1 cup reserved cooking water to sauté pan with miso mixture and whisk until well combined. Add noodles and butter and cook over medium heat, tossing constantly with tongs, until creamy sauce forms and noodles are well coated with sauce, about 1 minute. Turn off heat and slide pan to cool burner.

5. Add Pecorino and use tongs to toss until well combined. If sauce is too thick, adding remaining cooking water, a little at a time, to loosen. Serve with extra Pecorino.

From Chef Ken: A Starchy Secret

Surprise! The secret to creamy cacio e pepe is . . . the water you cook the noodles in. That cooking water is slightly salty and also full of starch from the pasta. The salt gives some extra seasoning while the starch thickens the sauce and gives it a smooth, creamy consistency (see "All About Emulsions," page 69)—it also helps our sauce stick to the noodles, so you get maximum flavor in every bite.

Pad See Ew

Pad see ew is a Thai stir-fry that typically includes rice noodles, veggies, meat, and a savory sauce. It's not at all spicy, and it's full of excellent flavors and textures that all blend together perfectly. As you're eating, try to create the perfect bite with some noodles, a piece of steak, and a piece of broccoli, all together!

Prepare Ingredients

¾ cup water, plus hot tap water for soaking noodles

12 ounces wide rice noodles

2 tablespoons fish sauce

1 tablespoon gluten-free oyster sauce

1 tablespoon gluten-free tamari

1 teaspoon sesame oil

1½ tablespoons plus 1½ tablespoons vegetable oil, measured separately

8 ounces New York strip steak, sliced thin

½ small red onion, sliced (see page 17)

3 garlic cloves, peeled and chopped (see page 17)

¼ cup sugar

1½ cups broccoli florets, chopped

1 cup chopped fresh cilantro (see page 17)

Gather Cooking Equipment

▷ 3 bowls (1 large, 1 medium, 1 small)

▷ Colander

▷ 12-inch wok or 12-inch nonstick skillet

▷ Wooden spoon

▷ Tongs

Start Cooking!

1. Fill large bowl with hot tap water. Add noodles and let them soak until they turn opaque (white in color) and are flexible (see photo, below), about 30 minutes.

2. Place colander in sink and drain noodles well.

3. In small bowl, combine fish sauce, oyster sauce, tamari, sesame oil, and ¾ cup water.

4. In 12-inch wok, heat 1½ tablespoons oil over medium-high heat until shimmering, about 2 minutes (oil should be hot but not smoking; see page 18). Carefully add steak (ask an adult for help) and cook for 1 minute—DO NOT STIR. Continue to cook, stirring often with wooden spoon, until steak is browned and cooked through (no longer pink), about 2 minutes. Transfer steak to medium bowl.

5. Add remaining 1½ tablespoons oil to pan and return to medium-high heat. Add red onion and garlic and cook, stirring often, for 2 minutes. Stir in sugar and cook until it starts to lightly caramelize (turn light brown), about 1 minute.

6. Carefully add fish sauce mixture, broccoli, and drained noodles. Cook, using tongs to toss mixture, until broccoli is bright green and noodles are tender, about 4 minutes.

7. Add steak and any juices left in bowl, and toss to combine. Turn off heat. Sprinkle with cilantro. Serve.

How to Soak Wide Rice Noodles

Fill large bowl with hot tap water. Add noodles and let them soak until they turn opaque (white in color) and are flexible, about 30 minutes.

Rice Vermicelli with Chicken and Coconut Curry

When my family was living in Paris for a little while, my parents would take us for Vietnamese food whenever they wanted a break from eating French food. (There is a large Vietnamese community in Paris and lots of Vietnamese restaurants.) They would order a bunch of different dishes, like crispy fried spring rolls, pork meatballs, fresh salads, and noodle soups similar to this one. The rule was that we had to try at least one bite of everything on the table. Those soups quickly became some of my favorites. The broth always has so much flavor and I've never met a noodle I didn't like. Thai curry paste can range from mild to spicy. Give yours a little taste and decide whether you want to use 2, 3, or 4 tablespoons, depending on how spicy you like it.

SERVES 4
TOTAL TIME 1¼ hours

Prepare Ingredients

½ cup vegetable oil

2–4 tablespoons Thai yellow curry paste

1 pound ground chicken

2 (15-ounce) cans coconut milk

⅓ cup fish sauce, plus extra for serving

¼ cup sugar

2 cups plus 4 quarts water, measured separately

8 ounces rice vermicelli noodles

4 scallions, root ends trimmed and scallions sliced thin

1 cup fresh basil leaves, torn into pieces

1 cup fresh cilantro leaves, chopped (see page 17)

Lime wedges

Sriracha

Gather Cooking Equipment

▷ Dutch oven

▷ Wooden spoon

▷ Colander

▷ Large pot

▷ Tongs

▷ Serving bowls

▷ Ladle

Start Cooking!

1. In Dutch oven, combine oil and curry paste. Cook over medium heat, stirring occasionally with wooden spoon, until fragrant, about 3 minutes.

2. Add chicken and use wooden spoon to break up chicken into small pieces. Cook until chicken is no longer pink, about 4 minutes.

3. Add coconut milk, fish sauce, sugar, and 2 cups water. Bring to a boil. Reduce heat to low, and gently simmer (small bubbles should break occasionally across surface of mixture) until slightly thickened, about 45 minutes. Turn off heat.

4. While curry cooks, set colander in sink. Add remaining 4 quarts water to large pot. Bring to a boil over high heat. Turn off heat. Carefully add noodles to pot. Let sit, stirring occasionally with clean wooden spoon, until noodles are tender but still a bit chewy (see package directions for timing).

5. Ask an adult to drain noodles in colander in sink. Rinse well under cold water. Use tongs to divide noodles evenly among serving bowls.

6. When curry is ready, use ladle to divide curry evenly among bowls of noodles (noodles should be swimming in sauce). Sprinkle scallions, basil, and cilantro over top. Serve with lime wedges, sriracha, and extra fish sauce.

From Chef Ken: An Ode to Fish Sauce

 Verveine is deeply aware of my love for fish sauce. It's an amazing ingredient that, in my opinion, is underrated by lots of people—though it's a key part of many East Asian cuisines, such as in Thailand, Vietnam, and Indonesia. It's salty and deeply savory. And fish sauce is versatile: It can be used as both an ingredient, stirred into soups and sauces, and a condiment, sprinkled on top of a finished dish. You can add just a tiny bit for an umami boost, like in Spicy Sicilian Tuna Pasta (page 66) or use it as one of the main ingredients, as in this broth. (And, yes, fish sauce does have a strong smell right out of the bottle, but it becomes much more subtle once you mix it with other ingredients.)

Mushroom-Miso Risotto

If I had to choose one dish in this book that brings people together the most, it would have to be this risotto. My family loves it. My extended family loves it. I love cooking this with other people. We take turns stirring it and sneaking bites while it cooks. It even tastes like home. It's warm and thick without being heavy and it's full of umami, my dad's favorite taste (see page 14). If you can't find carnaroli rice you can use arborio rice instead. You can use ½ cup of water and a squeeze of lemon juice instead of the white wine, if you prefer.

Prepare Ingredients

1 cup boiling water

1 ounce dried porcini mushrooms (or any other dried wild mushrooms)

7 cups chicken broth

3 tablespoons extra-virgin olive oil

3 tablespoons plus 5 tablespoons unsalted butter, measured separately

1 large onion, peeled and chopped fine (see page 17)

2 garlic cloves, peeled and minced (see page 17)

2 cups carnaroli rice

2 tablespoons red miso paste

½ cup white wine (see note, below left)

¾ cup grated Parmesan cheese (1½ ounces), plus extra for serving

2 tablespoons chopped fresh parsley (see page 17)

Gather Cooking Equipment

▷ Liquid measuring cup

▷ Fine-mesh strainer

▷ Small bowl

▷ Wooden spoon

▷ Cutting board

▷ Chef's knife

▷ Large saucepan with lid

▷ Dutch oven

▷ Ladle

Start Cooking!

1. In liquid measuring cup, carefully combine boiling water and dried mushrooms (ask an adult for help). Let soak for 20 minutes. Place fine-mesh strainer over small bowl. Pour mushrooms into strainer and use wooden spoon to press on mushrooms to push liquid through strainer into bowl.

2. Transfer mushrooms to cutting board and set mushroom soaking liquid aside. Use chef's knife to coarsely chop mushrooms.

3. In large saucepan, combine chicken broth and reserved mushroom soaking liquid. Bring to a boil over high heat. Turn off heat and cover with lid to keep warm.

4. In Dutch oven, combine oil and 3 tablespoons butter. Cook over medium heat until butter melts. Add onion, garlic, and chopped mushrooms and cook, stirring occasionally with wooden spoon, until softened, 5 to 7 minutes.

5. Add rice and miso and stir to combine. Add wine and cook until liquid evaporates and mixture is dry, about 1 minute.

6. Add 2 ladles of broth mixture (about ¾ cup) to rice and bring to rapid simmer (small bubbles should break constantly across surface of mixture). Cook, stirring often, until most of liquid is absorbed, about 2 minutes.

7. Add 2 more ladles of broth mixture and repeat cooking and stirring until almost all liquid is absorbed. Continue to add broth mixture, 2 ladles at a time, and cook, stirring often, until rice is al dente (tender but still a bit chewy), about 15 minutes. Mixture should be a bit loose (you might not need all the broth mixture). Turn off heat.

8. Add Parmesan, parsley, and remaining 5 tablespoons butter and stir constantly until well combined and creamy. If risotto is too thick, stir in a little more broth mixture to loosen. Season with salt and pepper to taste (see page 15). Serve with extra Parmesan.

Paella

I still remember the first time I had paella . . . I almost fell into it! My dad was doing a cooking event in Wyoming and my family came along. He and some other chefs were cooking paella outside in a huge field, which happened to have a play structure on it. My brother and I (about ages 6 and 8 at the time) were playing on the monkey bars. At one point, Luca pointed down at the HUGE pan that was right underneath us, filled with rice and sausage and seafood and saffron. As we were swinging on the bars, I almost fell into it! Luckily, Luca helped me to hang on. Once we climbed down, I asked my dad what was in the pan. He explained what paella was and asked me to try it. It had some of the best flavors I had ever tasted—a mix of spicy and sweet. Here is a recipe for a simple paella that you can cook at home—just don't put it under monkey bars! You can use arroz de Calasparra if you can't find the bomba rice.

Prepare Ingredients

- 2 tablespoons extra-virgin olive oil, plus extra for serving
- 1 pound boneless, skinless chicken thighs, cut into 1-inch pieces
- ½ teaspoon kosher salt
- 8 ounces Spanish chorizo, sliced ¼ inch thick
- 1 cup bomba rice
- 2 tablespoons tomato paste
- 1 teaspoon paprika
  Pinch saffron (optional)
- 3 cups chicken broth
- ½ cup frozen peas, thawed
- 4 scallions, root ends trimmed and scallions chopped

Gather Cooking Equipment

- ▷ 14-inch paella pan or 12-inch nonstick skillet
- ▷ Wooden spoon

Start Cooking!

1. In 14-inch paella pan, heat oil over medium heat until shimmering, about 2 minutes (oil should be hot but not smoking; see page 18). Add chicken and salt and cook until chicken is just starting to turn white, about 2 minutes.

2. Add chorizo and cook, stirring occasionally with wooden spoon, for 1 minute. Stir in rice and cook for 1 minute. Stir in tomato paste, paprika, and saffron (if using) and cook until fragrant, about 30 seconds.

3. Add chicken broth. Increase heat to high and bring mixture to a boil. Cook for 5 minutes—DO NOT STIR!

4. Reduce heat to low and simmer (small bubbles should break often across surface of mixture) until rice absorbs all liquid, about 12 minutes—AGAIN, DO NOT STIR!

5. Turn heat up to high, and cook until crust forms (see "Socarrat = Crispy Rice!," below), 2 to 4 minutes—STILL, DO NOT STIR! Turn off heat and slide pan to cool burner.

6. Sprinkle peas and scallions over top. Season with salt and pepper to taste (see page 15) and drizzle with extra oil. Serve with clean wooden spoon, making sure to scrape bottom of pan to get the socarrat.

From Chef Ken: Socarrat = Crispy Rice!

Socarrat is the name for the crispy, browned layer of rice that forms on the bottom of the pan as the paella cooks—it's the most prized part of the dish! To help the soccarat form, it's really important NOT to stir the rice once it starts cooking. This gives the bottom layer of rice lots of contact time with the hot surface of the paella pan, letting it get perfectly brown and crisp.

Eat with Your Hands

Crispy, Cheesy Quesadillas

We lived in Paris for almost a year when I was in fourth grade. When we were there, I used to get savory crepes from a spot that would put a layer of cheese on the outside of the crepe. The cheese on the outside would get supercrispy, and the cheese on the inside would get all melty, so you'd get two kinds of cheese with each bite. I could eat those crepes every day for the rest of my life. My dad created these quesadillas to mimic them, and they're just as good. The combo of a crunchy layer of cheese on the outside and the gooey cheese on the inside is perfect.

Prepare Ingredients

1 cup shredded Monterey Jack cheese (4 ounces)

⅔ cup shredded cheddar cheese (2½ ounces)

1 teaspoon extra-virgin olive oil

4 (6-inch) corn tortillas

Toppings, such as Charred Tomato Salsa (page 105) or your favorite salsa, guacamole, and/or sour cream

Gather Cooking Equipment

▷ Large plate

▷ Paper towels

▷ Medium bowl

▷ 10-inch nonstick skillet

▷ Tongs

▷ Spatula

▷ Cutting board

▷ Chef's knife

Start Cooking!

1. Line large plate with paper towels and place on counter near stovetop. In medium bowl, combine Monterey Jack and cheddar.

2. In 10-inch nonstick skillet, heat oil over medium heat until shimmering, about 2 minutes (oil should be hot but not smoking; see page 18). Add 1 tortilla and cook until just beginning to brown, 1 to 2 minutes (do not flip tortilla). Use tongs to transfer tortilla to paper towel–lined plate. Repeat cooking with 1 additional tortilla and transfer to plate.

3. Sprinkle one-quarter of cheese mixture directly onto surface of skillet, forming circle a little larger than size of tortilla. Place 1 cooked tortilla on top of cheese, and sprinkle another one-quarter of cheese over tortilla. Place 1 uncooked tortilla on top.

4. Cook until cheese on bottom is browned, 2 to 3 minutes. Use spatula to lift up edge of cheese, then slide spatula completely underneath quesadilla and carefully flip. Cook until cheese in between tortillas melts, about 2 minutes. Transfer quesadilla to paper towel–lined plate.

5. Repeat cooking in steps 3 and 4 with remaining cheese and tortillas to make 1 more quesadilla.

6. Transfer quesadillas to cutting board. Use chef's knife to cut quesadillas into wedges. Serve with toppings.

From Chef Ken: The Magic of Crispy Cheese

To me, the best part of a grilled cheese sandwich or quesadilla . . . or savory crepe . . . is when some of the cheese oozes out during cooking and gets crispy on the surface of the pan. Which gave me an idea: What if you could make a whole layer of crispy cheese that's actually part of your quesadilla, instead of just a happy accident? In this recipe, I sprinkle half the cheese right onto the hot skillet, where it can get nice and crispy—and it can stick to the tortilla. Then, I put the rest of the cheese inside the quesadilla, where it becomes melty and gooey. For Verveine and me, this is the perfect ratio of crispy to gooey cheese—and I'm pretty sure you'll think so too.

advanced

Steak Tacos

Taco Tuesdays. We've had them. You've had them. We've all had them. This is a recipe for the best kind of taco for your next Taco Tuesday. It's simple but has complex flavors, and you can put any toppings you want on top. I'm such a meat eater, and steak is my absolute favorite type of meat for tacos. There are two types of grills, charcoal and gas. We developed this recipe for a gas grill, which is easier and safer for kids to use. (And remember: Pretty much any day is a Tuesday if you want it to be.)

SERVES 4 to 6 (Makes 12 tacos)
TOTAL TIME 45 minutes, plus 1 hour marinating time

Prepare Ingredients

STEAK

¾ cup cola

½ onion, peeled and cut into quarters

2 tablespoons extra-virgin olive oil

2 garlic cloves, peeled (see page 17)

2 tablespoons gluten-free tamari

1½ pounds skirt or flank steak, cut in half crosswise (the short way) if steak is long

Vegetable oil

TACOS

½ teaspoon vegetable oil

12 (6-inch) corn tortillas

1 recipe Charred Tomato Salsa (page 105) or your favorite salsa

Chopped avocado

Shredded cheddar cheese

Chopped fresh cilantro (see page 17)

Gather Cooking Equipment

▷ Blender

▷ Dish towel

▷ Large zipper-lock plastic bag

▷ Gas grill

▷ Metal grill brush

▷ Tongs

▷ Paper towels

▷ Rimmed baking sheet

▷ Instant-read thermometer

▷ Cutting board

▷ 12-inch cast-iron skillet or 12-inch nonstick skillet

▷ Chef's knife

Start Cooking!

1. FOR THE STEAK: Add cola, onion, extra-virgin olive oil, garlic, and tamari to blender jar. Place lid on top of blender and hold lid firmly in place with folded dish towel. Turn on blender and process until mixture is smooth, about 1 minute. Stop blender and remove lid.

2. Place steak in large zipper-lock plastic bag and pour cola mixture over steak. Wash your hands. Seal bag, squeezing out as much air as possible. Place in refrigerator to marinate for at least 1 hour or up to 24 hours (the longer the better!).

3. When you're ready to cook, heat grill (ask an adult for help). Turn all burners to high; cover grill; and heat grill until hot, about 15 minutes. Leave all burners on high. Ask an adult to clean and oil cooking grate: Use metal grill brush to clean cooking grate. Use tongs to dip wad of paper towels in vegetable oil, and repeatedly brush grate with well-oiled paper towels until grate is black and glossy, 5 to 10 times.

4. Remove steak from zipper-lock bag and place on rimmed baking sheet; discard marinade. Pat steak dry with paper towels. Wash your hands.

5. Use tongs to transfer steak to grill. Cook until charred (well browned) on first side, 3 to 6 minutes. Use tongs to flip steak. Cook until charred and steak registers 125 degrees on instant-read thermometer (see page 18), 3 to 6 minutes. Transfer steak to cutting board. Turn off grill. Let steak rest for 5 minutes.

6. FOR THE TACOS: While steak rests, add ½ teaspoon oil to 12-inch cast-iron skillet. Use paper towel to spread oil evenly over bottom of skillet.

7. Heat skillet over medium heat until hot, about 2 minutes. Add 3 tortillas in single layer and cook for 1 minute. Use tongs to flip tortillas and continue to cook until warmed through and pliable, about 1 minute. Transfer tortillas to clean dish towel and wrap to keep warm. Repeat with remaining tortillas. Turn off heat.

8. Use chef's knife to slice steak thin against grain (see photo, page 104). Season with salt to taste (see page 15). Divide steak evenly among tortillas. Serve with salsa, chopped avocado, cheddar, and cilantro.

Keep Going!

From Chef Ken: Soda in Your Steak?

When you saw the first ingredient in this recipe (cola!), you might have wondered what soda was doing in a steak taco recipe. While it might be surprising, it actually makes sense when you break down the science behind it. First, cola is full of flavors, such as citrus, caramel, vanilla, and even a hint of cinnamon. It's also sugary, so it adds a bit of sweetness to our marinade. Just think: To get the same flavor, you'd have to prep and measure a whole bunch of other ingredients. Finally, cola is acidic (lemon juice and vinegar are other examples of acidic foods), and marinating in acidic ingredients help make meat, such as our steak, nice and tender.

How to Slice Steak Against the Grain

If you look closely at a piece of beef, you'll see little lines that run along the meat. This is called the "grain" because it looks like the grain, or lines, on a piece of wood. Slicing tougher cuts of beef, such as skirt steak, against (across) the grain makes them easier to chew. Use a chef's knife to slice your steak thin against the grain.

MAKES 1½ cups
TOTAL TIME 30 minutes

Charred Tomato Salsa

Prepare Ingredients

5	plum tomatoes
½	small onion, peeled and cut into 2 wedges
1	garlic clove, peeled (see page 17)
½	cup fresh cilantro leaves
1	tablespoon lime juice, squeezed from ½ lime
1½	teaspoons kosher salt

Gather Cooking Equipment

▷ 12-inch cast-iron skillet or 12-inch nonstick skillet

▷ Tongs

▷ Food processor

▷ Fine-mesh strainer

▷ Serving bowl

Start Cooking!

1. Heat 12-inch cast-iron skillet over medium heat until hot, about 2 minutes. Use tongs to add whole tomatoes, onion wedges, and garlic to skillet. Cook, turning vegetables occasionally with tongs, until charred and burned slightly, 10 to 15 minutes. Turn off heat.

2. Transfer charred vegetables to food processor. Add cilantro, lime juice, and salt. Lock lid into place. Hold down pulse button for 1 second, then release. Repeat until salsa has chunky consistency, eight to ten 1-second pulses.

3. Remove lid and carefully remove processor blade (ask an adult for help). Set fine-mesh strainer over serving bowl. Transfer salsa to strainer and let drain for 30 to 60 seconds. Discard liquid in bowl. Transfer salsa to now-empty bowl and serve. (Salsa can be refrigerated in airtight storage container for up to 3 days.)

Fish Tacos

My family has spent a lot of time by the water, like here in Boston or up in Maine, so I've eaten a lot of fish in my life. And my favorite way to eat fish is in a taco. The fish we use in these tacos, particularly cod or branzino, is really light and doesn't taste too fishy. (My brother is very particular about fish, and he definitely approves of these fish tacos!) We love squeezing thick, tangy Kewpie mayo on our fish tacos, too, but you can use regular mayonnaise, if desired.

SERVES 4 to 6 (Makes 12 tacos)
TOTAL TIME 1¼ hours

Prepare Ingredients

FISH

½ cup chopped fresh cilantro (see page 17), plus extra for serving

¼ cup extra-virgin olive oil

2 tablespoons lemon juice, squeezed from 1 lemon

1 tablespoon maple syrup

2 garlic cloves, peeled and chopped (see page 17)

1 teaspoon paprika

1 teaspoon ground cumin

1 teaspoon gluten-free tamari

1 teaspoon fish sauce

½ teaspoon hot sauce

1½ pounds skinless cod, branzino, or salmon fillets (about 6 ounces each)

TACOS

½ teaspoon vegetable oil

12 (6-inch) corn tortillas

1 recipe Charred Tomato Salsa (see page 105) or your favorite salsa

Guacamole

Shredded romaine lettuce

Kewpie mayonnaise (see note, below left)

Gather Cooking Equipment

▷ Rimmed baking sheet
▷ Aluminum foil
▷ Medium bowl
▷ Rubber spatula
▷ Instant-read thermometer
▷ Oven mitts
▷ Cooling rack
▷ 12-inch cast-iron skillet or 12-inch nonstick skillet
▷ Paper towel
▷ Tongs
▷ Dish towel
▷ 2 forks

Start Cooking!

1. FOR THE FISH: Line rimmed baking sheet with aluminum foil. In medium bowl, combine cilantro, extra-virgin olive oil, lemon juice, syrup, garlic, paprika, cumin, tamari, fish sauce, and hot sauce. Stir with rubber spatula until well combined.

2. Place fish on foil-lined baking sheet. Pour cilantro mixture over fish and turn fish in sauce until well coated. Wash your hands. Place baking sheet in refrigerator for at least 15 minutes or up to 1 hour.

3. Meanwhile, adjust oven rack to middle position and heat oven to 450 degrees.

4. When fish is ready, place baking sheet in oven. Bake until center of cod or branzino registers 140 degrees or center of salmon registers 125 degrees on instant-read thermometer (see page 18), 8 to 15 minutes.

5. Use oven mitts to remove baking sheet from oven and place on cooling rack (ask an adult for help). Carefully cover baking sheet loosely with foil (baking sheet will be HOT).

6. FOR THE TACOS: Add vegetable oil to 12-inch cast-iron skillet. Use paper towel to spread oil evenly over bottom of skillet.

7. Heat skillet over medium heat until hot, about 2 minutes. Add 3 tortillas in single layer and cook for 1 minute. Use tongs to flip tortillas and continue to cook until warmed through and pliable, about 1 minute. Transfer tortillas to clean dish towel and wrap to keep warm. Repeat with remaining tortillas. Turn off heat.

8. Use 2 forks to flake fish into large chunks on baking sheet. Season with salt to taste (see page 15). Divide fish evenly among tortillas. Top with salsa, guacamole, lettuce, mayonnaise, and cilantro. Serve.

Sopes

My dad used to come to my school and make sopes for my class (another benefit of having a chef for a dad!). Before he would arrive, my friends would ask me what sopes are because they weren't familiar with them, and I'd describe them as "thick tacos." These fried corn pillows are crispy and they're a great vehicle for toppings—and you can top them with pretty much anything you feel like. My favorites are steak or guacamole. We developed this recipe with the Maseca brand of masa harina. If you use other brands, your dough might be slightly wetter.

4 **SERVES** 2 to 3 (Makes 6 sopes)
TOTAL TIME 45 minutes

Prepare Ingredients

1 cup (4 ounces) masa harina

½ teaspoon kosher salt

¾ cup (6 ounces) hot tap water

½ cup vegetable oil for frying

Toppings, such as Charred Tomato Salsa (page 105) or your favorite salsa, guacamole, chopped avocado, sour cream, and/or shredded cheddar cheese

Gather Cooking Equipment

▷ Medium bowl

▷ Fork

▷ Plastic wrap

▷ Scissors

▷ Large zipper-lock plastic bag

▷ Pie plate

▷ Ruler

▷ 2 rimmed baking sheets

▷ Paper towels

▷ 12-inch skillet

▷ 2 spatulas

Start Cooking!

1. In medium bowl, use fork to stir together masa harina and salt. Add hot water and mix until mixture starts to form dough. Use your hands to knead dough in bowl until ball forms, about 1 minute. Cover bowl with plastic wrap and let sit for at least 15 minutes or up to 24 hours (if leaving for more than 1 hour, place bowl in refrigerator).

2. While dough rests, use scissors to cut side seams of large zipper-lock plastic bag, leaving bottom seam intact.

3. When dough is ready, divide dough into 6 equal portions. Roll each portion into ball. Shape sopes following photos, below.

4. Line second rimmed baking sheet with double layer of paper towels and place near stovetop. In 12-inch skillet, heat oil over medium heat until shimmering, about 3 minutes (oil should be hot but not smoking; see page 18).

5. Carefully add 3 sopes to skillet (ask an adult for help). Fry until golden brown and crispy on first side, 2 to 4 minutes. Use 2 spatulas to carefully flip sopes (ask an adult for help). Cook until golden brown and crispy on second side, 2 to 4 minutes. Transfer sopes to paper towel–lined baking sheet.

6. Repeat frying in step 5 with remaining sopes. Turn off heat. Serve sopes with toppings.

How to Shape Sopes

1. Open zipper-lock plastic bag, place 1 ball inside, and fold top of bag over ball. Place pie plate on top of bag and press ball into 4-inch circle, about ¼ inch thick.

2. Lift up top of plastic bag. Use your hands to create lip of dough around edge. Transfer sope to rimmed baking sheet. Repeat shaping with remaining 5 dough balls.

intermediate

Chicken Taquitos

One morning, when we were on vacation in Puerto Rico, my dad made us these taquitos for breakfast (don't ask me why!). I had never seen anything like them before and he explained that taquitos are like crispy, rolled-up tacos, with the filling on the inside. They immediately became one of my favorite meals and, since then, I've probably eaten them about a thousand times for dinner, lunch, and yes, even breakfast!

SERVES 4 to 6 (Makes 12 taquitos)
TOTAL TIME 2 hours

Prepare Ingredients

1   pound boneless, skinless chicken thighs

1½   teaspoons kosher salt

¼   teaspoon pepper

6   tablespoons extra-virgin olive oil

1   small onion, peeled and chopped fine (see page 17)

2   garlic cloves, peeled and minced (see page 17)

1   (14-ounce) can crushed tomatoes

1   cup chicken broth

1   cup chopped fresh cilantro (see page 17)

1   tablespoon minced canned chipotle pepper in adobo

1   teaspoon dried oregano

¾   cup shredded cheddar cheese (3 ounces)

12   (6-inch) corn tortillas

Toppings, such as Charred Tomato Salsa (page 105) or your favorite salsa, guacamole, sour cream, and/or shredded cheddar cheese

Gather Cooking Equipment

▷ 3 plates (2 large, 1 microwave-safe)

▷ Paper towels

▷ Large saucepan

▷ Tongs

▷ Wooden spoon

▷ Cutting board

▷ 2 forks

▷ Medium bowl

▷ Ladle

▷ Liquid measuring cup

▷ 2 dish towels

▷ Serving platter

▷ 12-inch nonstick skillet

Start Cooking!

1. Place chicken on large plate. Use paper towels to pat chicken dry. Sprinkle salt and pepper evenly over both sides of chicken. Wash your hands.

2. In large saucepan, heat 2 tablespoons oil over medium heat until shimmering, about 2 minutes (oil should be hot but not smoking; see page 18). Use tongs to add chicken to saucepan. Cook until browned on first side, 5 to 7 minutes. Use tongs to flip chicken and cook until browned on second side, 5 to 7 minutes.

3. Add onion and garlic and cook, stirring occasionally with wooden spoon, until onion is softened, about 5 minutes.

4. Stir in tomatoes, broth, cilantro, chipotle pepper, and oregano, scraping bottom of saucepan. Bring mixture to simmer (small bubbles should break often across surface of mixture). Reduce heat to medium-low and simmer until chicken is very tender, about 30 minutes. Turn off heat.

5. Use clean tongs to transfer chicken to cutting board and let cool slightly. Use 2 forks to shred chicken into bite-size pieces (see photo, page 112).

Keep Going!

6. Transfer shredded chicken to medium bowl. Use ladle to measure ¼ cup cooked tomato sauce and add to bowl with chicken. Add cheese and stir until well combined. Season with salt and pepper to taste (see page 15).

7. Wrap 6 tortillas in damp dish towel and place on microwave-safe plate. Heat in microwave until warm and flexible, 1 to 1½ minutes. Fill and roll 6 taquitos following photos, right. Repeat step 7 with remaining tortillas and filling.

8. Line serving platter with paper towels and place near stovetop. In 12-inch nonstick skillet, heat 2 tablespoons oil over medium heat until shimmering, about 2 minutes. Use clean tongs to carefully add 6 taquitos, seam side down.

9. Cook until crispy on first side, about 3 minutes. Use tongs to flip taquitos and cook until crispy on second side, 2 to 3 minutes. Transfer to paper–towel lined serving platter.

10. Repeat cooking with remaining 2 tablespoons oil and remaining 6 taquitos and transfer to serving platter. Turn off heat. Serve warm with extra cooked tomato sauce and toppings.

How to Shred Chicken

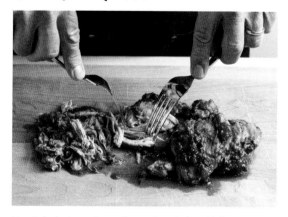

Use 2 forks to pull meat apart and shred it into bite-size pieces.

How to Shape Taquitos

1. Lay 6 warm tortillas on clean counter. Divide half of filling evenly among tortillas.

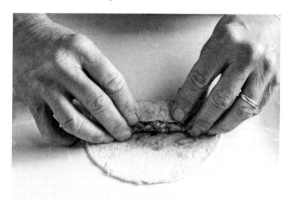

2. Roll tortillas around filling into tight logs. Place rolled tortillas seam-side down on second large plate. Cover rolled tortillas with second damp dish towel to prevent them from drying out.

A Heated Debate

 Wow, this chapter really has a lot of corn-y recipes in it.

 Yeah, we've got tacos, sopes, arepas, pupusas, and these taquitos.

 Let's rank them . . . how would you do it?

 I'd say tacos are my favorite, and then sopes, taquitos, pupusas, and finally, arepas.

 Mine are sopes, arepas, tacos, pupusas, and then taquitos in last place. It's hard though—I love them all!

Fresh Corn Arepas

I love the spirit and tradition of carnivals and I love carnival foods. Every summer we go to this carnival in Coney Island, New York, which is where I fell in love with arepas. I am always excited to eat these slightly sweet, savory corn cakes. They're perfect to eat with your hands, whether you're at a carnival or somewhere else. Arepas are great on their own, with some butter, or with sour cream, salsa, and grilled meats. You can even eat them for breakfast! For information on substituting gluten-free flours, see page 12.

SERVES 4 to 6 (Makes 8 arepas)
TOTAL TIME 45 minutes

Prepare Ingredients

¾ cup fresh or frozen corn (thawed, if frozen)

½ cup (4 ounces) whole-milk ricotta cheese

½ cup grated Parmesan cheese (1 ounce)

1 cup (5 ounces) masarepa

¾ cup (6 ounces) whole milk

⅓ cup (1⅔ ounces) Cup4Cup Gluten-Free Multipurpose Flour

4 tablespoons unsalted butter, melted (see page 16)

2 tablespoons sugar

1 tablespoon honey

1 teaspoon baking powder

1 teaspoon kosher salt

1 tablespoon plus 1 tablespoon extra-virgin olive oil, measured separately

Vegetable oil spray

Gather Cooking Equipment

▷ Food processor

▷ Rubber spatula

▷ Medium bowl

▷ Plastic wrap

▷ Rimmed baking sheet

▷ Paper towels

▷ 12-inch nonstick skillet

▷ ¼-cup dry measuring cup

▷ Spatula

Start Cooking!

1. Add corn, ricotta, and Parmesan to food processor. Lock lid into place. Turn on processor and process until corn is broken down and mixture is combined, about 1 minute. Stop processor and remove lid.

2. Add masarepa, milk, flour, melted butter, sugar, honey, baking powder, and salt. Lock lid back into place. Turn on processor and process until smooth, about 1 minute. Stop processor. Remove lid and carefully remove processor blade (ask an adult for help).

3. Use rubber spatula to scrape batter into medium bowl. Cover with plastic wrap and let sit for 15 minutes.

4. Line rimmed baking sheet with double layer of paper towels and place near stovetop. In 12-inch nonstick skillet, heat 1 tablespoon oil over medium-low heat until shimmering, about 2 minutes (oil should be hot but not smoking; see page 18).

5. Spray ¼-cup dry measuring cup with vegetable oil spray. Use greased measuring cup to scoop heaping ¼ cup batter into skillet. Repeat 3 more times, leaving space between portions.

6. Cook until golden brown on first side, 2 to 3 minutes. Use spatula to flip arepas. Cook until golden brown on second side, 2 to 3 minutes. (If skillet starts to smoke, turn heat down.) Transfer arepas to paper towel-lined baking sheet.

7. Add remaining 1 tablespoon oil to skillet and repeat cooking in steps 5 and 6 with remaining batter to make 4 more arepas. Turn off heat. Serve.

ABOUT AREPAS

Arepas are very popular in Venezuela and Colombia—this recipe is closer to the Colombian style.

In Colombia, arepas are usually eaten whole.

In Venezuela, you'll see arepas split in half and filled with chicken, avocado, beef, and more.

Zucchini Pupusas

In East Boston, there is a restaurant that serves the best pupusas. We used to go there a lot, particularly when we had a half day of school and my dad would pick me up. When I found out that pupusas were naturally gluten-free, I was so excited to make them at home, too. We developed this recipe using the Maseca brand of masa harina. If you use other brands, start with 1 cup (8 ounces) of water and add more to your dough as needed.

SERVES 3 to 6 (Makes 6 pupusas)
TOTAL TIME 1 hour

Prepare Ingredients

FILLING

1½	teaspoons extra-virgin olive oil
½	cup shredded zucchini (about ½ small zucchini)
	Pinch pepper
⅛	teaspoon kosher salt
1	cup shredded mozzarella cheese (4 ounces)
1–2	tablespoons chopped jarred jalapeño chile slices

DOUGH

1½	cups (6 ounces) masa harina
1¼	cups (10 ounces) water, plus extra if needed
¾	teaspoon kosher salt
1	teaspoon plus 1 teaspoon extra-virgin olive oil, measured separately, plus extra for shaping

Gather Cooking Equipment

▷ 10-inch skillet

▷ Wooden spoon

▷ Colander

▷ 2 medium bowls

▷ Plastic wrap

▷ Ruler

▷ 1-tablespoon measuring spoon

▷ 2 rimmed baking sheets

▷ 2 cooling racks

▷ 12-inch cast-iron skillet or 12-inch nonstick skillet

▷ Oven mitts

▷ Spatula

Start Cooking!

1. FOR THE FILLING: In 10-inch skillet, heat 1½ teaspoons oil over medium heat until shimmering, about 2 minutes (oil should be hot but not smoking; see page 18). Add zucchini, pepper, and ⅛ teaspoon salt and cook, stirring occasionally with wooden spoon, until wilted, about 1 minute. Turn off heat.

2. Place colander in sink. Transfer zucchini to colander (ask an adult for help). Let cool completely, about 10 minutes. Transfer zucchini to medium bowl. Add mozzarella and jalapeños and stir to combine.

3. FOR THE DOUGH: In second medium bowl, combine masa harina, water, and ¾ teaspoon salt. Stir with clean wooden spoon until combined. Use your hands to knead mixture until dough forms, about 1 minute. (If many large cracks form when dough is squeezed, stir in more water, 1 teaspoon at a time, until dough no longer cracks when pressed.)

4. Divide dough into 6 equal portions, roll into balls, and place on counter. Cover dough balls with plastic wrap. Shape and fill pupusas following photos, page 118.

5. Adjust oven rack to middle position and heat oven to 200 degrees. Set cooling rack in second rimmed baking sheet.

6. Heat 12-inch cast-iron skillet over medium-low heat until hot, about 3 minutes. Add 1 teaspoon oil to skillet. Hold skillet handle with oven mitts and swirl to coat skillet with oil (ask an adult for help).

7. Add 3 pupusas to skillet and cook until well browned on first side, 4 to 6 minutes. Use spatula to flip pupusas. Cook until well browned on second side, 4 to 6 minutes. Transfer to rack set in rimmed baking sheet and place in oven to keep warm.

8. Repeat cooking with remaining oil and pupusas. Use oven mitts to remove baking sheet from oven and place on second cooling rack (ask an adult for help). Serve.

 Keep Going!

How to Shape Pupusas

1. Working with 1 dough ball at a time, use your hands to shape dough into 4-inch circle, about ½ inch thick.

2. Scoop 2 tablespoons filling into center of dough, pull sides over filling, and pinch at top. Roll into smooth ball. Repeat with remaining dough and filling.

3. Lightly grease your hands with oil. Working with 1 filled dough ball at a time, gently flatten dough with your hands into 4½-inch circle, about ½ inch thick.

4. Place on rimmed baking sheet and cover with plastic wrap. Repeat flattening with remaining filled dough balls.

Two Corn Flours

These pupusas use masa harina, but arepas use masarepa. They're both made from corn. Can't we just use the same flour for both recipes?

You can't. They're too different. Masarepa is made from corn that's been cooked, dried, and ground up. For masa harina, the corn is nixtamalized before it's ground into a flour.

Nixtama-what?

"Nixtamalized" means the corn was soaked in an alkaline solution. It gives masa harina that iconic "corn chip" smell and flavor.

Ohhh . . . that's why corn tortillas and tortilla chips and pupusas all smell similar.

Cheesy Gougères

My mom makes these for Christmas parties, and I always help. Everyone loves them because, I mean, who doesn't love airy, puffy, delicious, cheesy clouds of bread? I know you'll love them, too. For information on substituting gluten-free flours, see page 12.

MAKES 20 to 24 gougères
TOTAL TIME 1 hour

Prepare Ingredients

½ cup (2½ ounces) Cup4Cup Gluten-Free Multipurpose Flour

¼ cup cornstarch

⅓ cup (2⅔ ounces) whole milk

⅓ cup (2⅔ ounces) water

4 tablespoons unsalted butter

¾ teaspoon sugar

¼ teaspoon kosher salt

3 large eggs

½ cup shredded Gruyère (1½ ounces) or 1 cup grated Parmesan cheese (2 ounces)

Gather Cooking Equipment

▷ Rimmed baking sheet

▷ Parchment paper

▷ Small bowl

▷ Medium saucepan

▷ Wooden spoon

▷ Stand mixer with paddle attachment

▷ Rubber spatula

▷ 1-tablespoon measuring spoon

▷ Oven mitts

▷ Cooling rack

Start Cooking!

1. Adjust oven rack to middle position and heat oven to 375 degrees. Line rimmed baking sheet with parchment paper.

2. In small bowl, combine flour and cornstarch; set aside. In medium saucepan, combine milk, water, butter, sugar, and salt. Bring to simmer over medium heat (small bubbles should break often across surface of mixture). Turn off heat.

3. Add flour mixture to saucepan and use wooden spoon to stir until combined. Cook over low heat and stir until dough starts to ball together and turns dry around edges, about 1 minute (see photo, below). Turn off heat.

4. Transfer dough to bowl of stand mixer (ask an adult for help). Lock bowl into place and attach paddle to stand mixer. Let dough cool for 5 minutes.

5. Start mixer on medium-low speed. Add eggs, one at a time, and beat until combined, stopping mixer and using rubber spatula to scrape down bowl after adding each egg. Increase speed to medium-high and beat until smooth, about 2 minutes.

6. Stop mixer and add Gruyère. Start mixer on medium speed and beat until combined, about 1 minute. Stop mixer. Remove bowl from stand mixer.

7. Portion and shape gougères following photos, page 122.

8. Place baking sheet in oven and bake until golden brown, 20 to 25 minutes. Use oven mitts to transfer baking sheet to cooling rack (ask an adult for help). Serve hot!

 Keep Going!

How to Cook Gougères Dough

Add flour mixture to saucepan and use wooden spoon to stir until combined. Cook over low heat and stir until dough starts to ball together and turns dry around edges, about 1 minute.

How to Portion and Shape Gougères

1. Scoop 1 heaping tablespoon of dough onto parchment-lined baking sheet, using your finger to scrape out dough as needed. Repeat to make 20 to 24 mounds of dough, leaving space between mounds.

2. Lightly wet your finger and gently smooth tops of mounds.

ONE DOUGH, LOTS OF DELICIOUSNESS

This unique, cooked dough is called pate a choux ("pat uh shoo"). It's fun to say and even more fun to eat. (Fun fact: "Pate a choux" is French for "cabbage paste," named for the shape it bakes into when you're making cream puffs or gougères.) Believe it or not, this one dough forms the base for lots of sweet and savory dishes . . .

Éclairs

Gougères

Cream Puffs

Gnocchi à la Parisienne

Churros

Socca

My mom makes these chickpea pancakes for my brother and me, with extra-virgin olive oil and rosemary and Parmesan. If she had called them chickpea flour pancakes when we were little, we never would have tried them. But she just called them "socca" and we loved them. I promise you'll love the unique flavor and texture of these delicious pancakes!

4 🔳 🔳 **SERVES** 2 to 4 (Makes 4 socca)
TOTAL TIME 45 minutes

Prepare Ingredients

1 cup plus 2 tablespoons (5 ounces) chickpea flour

1 cup (8 ounces) water

¾ teaspoon kosher salt

1 tablespoon plus 4 teaspoons extra-virgin olive oil, measured separately, plus extra for drizzling

½ teaspoon chopped fresh rosemary, plus extra for serving (see page 17)

¼ cup grated Parmesan cheese (½ ounce), plus extra for serving

Gather Cooking Equipment

▷ Large bowl

▷ Whisk

▷ Measuring spoons

▷ 10-inch cast-iron skillet or 10-inch nonstick skillet

▷ Oven mitts

▷ ⅓-cup dry measuring cup

▷ Spatula

▷ Rimmed baking sheet

▷ Cooling rack

▷ Cutting board

▷ Chef's knife

Start Cooking!

1. Adjust oven rack to middle position and heat oven to 200 degrees. In large bowl, whisk chickpea flour, water, salt, and 1 tablespoon oil until well combined.

2. Add 1 teaspoon oil to 10-inch cast-iron skillet. Heat skillet over medium heat until hot, about 3 minutes (2 minutes if using nonstick skillet). Hold skillet handle with oven mitts and swirl to coat skillet with oil (ask an adult for help).

3. Add pinch rosemary to oil, then add ⅓ cup batter to skillet. Cook until deep golden brown, 5 to 7 minutes.

4. Use spatula to flip socca. Sprinkle 1 tablespoon Parmesan over socca. Cook until deep golden brown on second side and crispy on edges, 5 to 7 minutes. Transfer socca to rimmed baking sheet and place in oven to keep warm.

5. Repeat cooking in steps 2–4 with remaining oil, rosemary, batter, and Parmesan to make 3 more socca, transferring each one to baking sheet in oven. (If socca are browning too quickly, reduce heat to medium-low.) Turn off heat.

6. Use oven mitts to remove baking sheet from oven and place on cooling rack (ask an adult for help). Transfer socca to cutting board and use chef's knife to cut into wedges. Drizzle with extra oil and sprinkle with extra rosemary and Parmesan. Serve.

From Chef Ken: International Pancakes

In the city of Nice and across the south of France, you'll see street vendors selling hot, crispy socca. But France isn't the only country to make savory pancakes from chickpea flour. In Italy, a similar recipe is called "farinata," "torta di ceci" (literally "chickpea cake"), or "cecia." On the other side of the world, in Uruguay and Argentina, you might eat a version called "fainá" with a sauce or dip or even alongside a slice of pizza. The dish was brought to South America by Italian immigrants.

Crêpes au Citron

I love everything about crepes. I love getting them at random places in Paris. I love making them with my grandma. I love cooking them in the morning for my family. I love the sound of pouring the batter into the pan. I love filling them with all kinds of ingredients. And I've tried just about everything, from chocolate-hazelnut spread to strawberries for sweet crepes or canned tuna to salmon if I'm going savory. For information on substituting gluten-free flours, see page 12.

SERVES 3 to 6 (Makes 6 crepes)
TOTAL TIME 45 minutes, plus 1 hour resting time

Prepare Ingredients

¾ cup (6 ounces) milk

½ cup (2½ ounces) Cup4Cup Gluten-Free Multipurpose Flour

2 large eggs

⅛ teaspoon kosher salt

2 tablespoons plus 2 tablespoons unsalted butter, measured separately, melted and cooled (see page 16)

1½ teaspoons plus 2 tablespoons sugar, measured separately

2 tablespoons lemon juice, squeezed from 1 lemon

2 tablespoons unsalted butter, cut into 6 small cubes

Gather Cooking Equipment

▷ Blender

▷ Dish towel

▷ 2-cup liquid measuring cup

▷ Plastic wrap

▷ Rimmed baking sheet

▷ Parchment paper

▷ Pastry brush

▷ 10-inch nonstick skillet

▷ Spatula

▷ Plate

▷ 1-teaspoon measuring spoon

▷ Oven mitts

▷ Cooling rack

Start Cooking!

1. Add milk, flour, eggs, salt, 2 tablespoons melted butter, and 1½ teaspoons sugar to blender jar. Place lid on top of blender and hold lid firmly in place with folded dish towel. Turn on blender and process until smooth, about 1 minute. Stop blender and remove lid. Pour batter into liquid measuring cup, cover with plastic wrap, and place in refrigerator for at least 1 hour or up to 2 days.

2. Adjust oven rack to middle position and heat oven to 250 degrees. Line rimmed baking sheet with parchment paper.

3. Use pastry brush to coat bottom of 10-inch nonstick skillet with thin layer of melted butter. Heat skillet over medium heat until hot, about 2 minutes. Pour ¼ cup batter into skillet and tilt and swirl skillet to evenly coat bottom of skillet with batter.

4. Cook until crepe is just set, 1 to 2 minutes. Use spatula to flip crepe. Cook until golden brown, about 30 seconds. Slide crepe onto plate.

5. Repeat cooking to make 5 more crepes, brushing skillet in between each one with a little more melted butter and stacking finished crepes on plate.

6. Fill and fold top crepe following photo, below. Repeat filling and folding remaining 5 crepes with remaining sugar, lemon juice, and butter cubes.

7. Place baking sheet in oven and bake until butter is melted and crepes are hot, 3 to 5 minutes. Use oven mitts to remove baking sheet from oven and place on cooling rack (ask an adult for help). Serve.

How to Fill and Fold Crepes

Sprinkle top crepe with 1 teaspoon sugar, and drizzle with 1 teaspoon lemon juice. Use your hands to fold in all 4 sides to create square. Transfer crepe to parchment-lined baking sheet. Place 1 cube of butter in center of crepe.

Chapter 4

Meat, Poultry, and Seafood

"Food Court" Chicken

I love chicken because it's so versatile. It can be prepared in so many different ways—chicken shines in a good sauce, as nuggets, or in pasta. My experience with chicken started at the food court in the Prudential Center, a mall in Boston. They'd hand out samples of chicken from all the different food court restaurants, and I would turn it into a taste test to see what I liked the best. This recipe is based on my favorite chicken at the food court—tasty, crunchy, saucy fried chicken bits from The Panda Express. We love Frank's hot sauce in this recipe, but you can use your favorite hot sauce, if you like. Don't use stone-ground cornmeal here, it will make the coating too tough and crunchy.

4 ⊞⊞ **SERVES 4**
   ⊞⊞ **TOTAL TIME** 1 hour, plus 1 hour brining time

Prepare Ingredients

½ cup (4 ounces) buttermilk

1 tablespoon pickle brine (see "In a Pickle," below right)

1½ teaspoons hot sauce

1 garlic clove, peeled and chopped (see page 17)

1 pound boneless, skinless chicken thighs, cut into 1-inch pieces

½ cup (2½ ounces) potato starch

½ cup (2 ounces) cornstarch

½ cup (2½ ounces) white rice flour

1 tablespoon fine-ground cornmeal

1 teaspoon kosher salt

½ teaspoon pepper

½ teaspoon onion powder

½ teaspoon paprika

4 cups vegetable oil for frying

¼ cup gluten-free teriyaki sauce, BBQ sauce, buffalo sauce, or honey-mustard sauce

Gather Cooking Equipment

▷ 2 bowls (1 large, 1 medium)

▷ Whisk

▷ Plastic wrap

▷ 2 cooling racks

▷ 2 rimmed baking sheets

▷ Tongs

▷ Paper towels

▷ Dutch oven

▷ Instant-read thermometer

▷ Spider skimmer or slotted spoon

▷ Serving bowl

▷ Rubber spatula

Start Cooking!

1. In medium bowl, whisk together buttermilk, pickle brine, hot sauce, and garlic. Add chicken to bowl. Wash your hands. Cover bowl with plastic wrap and place in refrigerator. Brine for at least 1 hour or up to 24 hours. Clean and dry whisk.

2. When chicken is ready, in large bowl, whisk together potato starch, cornstarch, white rice flour, cornmeal, salt, pepper, onion powder, and paprika. Place cooling rack inside rimmed baking sheet.

3. Remove bowl of chicken from refrigerator and discard plastic wrap. Working with 4 or 5 pieces of chicken at a time, use tongs to lift chicken out of brine, letting excess drip back into bowl. Transfer chicken to bowl of potato starch mixture. Toss chicken to coat all sides evenly. Transfer chicken to cooling rack set in rimmed baking sheet. Wash your hands.

4. Place second cooling rack inside second rimmed baking sheet and line with double layer of paper towels. Place on counter next to stovetop.

5. Heat oil in Dutch oven over medium-low heat until it registers 325 degrees on instant-read thermometer. Ask an adult to use spider skimmer to carefully add half of chicken to oil. Fry until chicken is golden brown, crispy, and cooked through, 4 to 6 minutes. Use spider skimmer to transfer chicken to paper towel–lined cooling rack.

6. Return oil to 325 degrees. Repeat frying with remaining chicken. Turn off heat. Let oil cool completely, then discard oil (ask an adult for help—never pour frying oil down the drain!).

7. Transfer chicken to serving bowl. Add sauce of your choice and use rubber spatula to gently toss until chicken is well coated. Season with salt to taste (see page 15). Serve.

From Chef Ken: In a Pickle

Just like the cola in our Steak Tacos (page 102), the pickle brine in this recipe brings a bunch of ingredients to the party. Pickle brine is the tangy, salty, flavor-packed liquid in a jar of pickles. It's usually made of vinegar, salt, sugar, and spices. Soaking the chicken in a mixture of buttermilk, pickle brine, garlic, and hot sauce does two things to our meat. As the mixture makes its way into the chicken, it seasons the meat all the way through. It also helps make the chicken tender and extra-juicy, thanks to the salt in the pickle brine and the acidic vinegar and buttermilk.

Chicken Milanesa

My grandma makes this thin, crispy breaded chicken dish for me all the time. Hers is the best. (But this version is a close second!) We're huge fans of Parmesan in my family. We always put mounds of Parmesan on our milanesas, so it looks like a little pile of snow, and I recommend you do the same. For information on substituting gluten-free flours, see page 12.

4 ⊞ **SERVES 4**
TOTAL TIME 45 minutes

Prepare Ingredients

4   (3- to 4-ounce) chicken cutlets,
    ½ inch thick

1   teaspoon kosher salt

1   cup (5 ounces) Cup4Cup
    Gluten-Free Multipurpose Flour

3   large eggs

1   cup gluten-free Italian bread
    crumbs

3   tablespoons grated Parmesan
    cheese, plus extra for serving

2   tablespoons chopped fresh
    parsley (see page 17)

1   cup extra-virgin olive oil for
    frying, plus extra for drizzling
    Lemon wedges

Gather Cooking Equipment

▷   2 large plates

▷   Paper towels

▷   3 shallow dishes

▷   Fork

▷   Tongs

▷   12-inch skillet

▷   Cooling rack

Start Cooking!

1. Place chicken cutlets on large plate. Pat chicken dry with paper towels. Sprinkle salt evenly over both sides of chicken. Wash your hands.

2. Spread flour in shallow dish. Place eggs in second shallow dish and beat with fork until well combined. In third shallow dish, toss bread crumbs, Parmesan, and parsley until well combined.

3. Working with 1 cutlet at a time, use tongs to bread cutlets following photos, below. Return breaded cutlets to large plate.

4. Line second large plate with triple layer of paper towels and place next to stovetop. In 12-inch skillet, heat oil over medium heat until shimmering, 3 to 5 minutes (oil should be hot but not smoking; see page 18).

5. Ask an adult to use clean tongs to carefully add 2 cutlets to skillet. Cook until golden on first side, about 4 minutes. Use tongs to carefully flip cutlets and cook until chicken is golden, crispy, and cooked through, about 4 minutes. Transfer chicken to paper towel–lined plate and let sit for 1 minute, then transfer to cooling rack.

6. Repeat frying with remaining 2 cutlets. Turn off heat. Let oil cool completely, then discard oil (ask an adult for help—never pour frying oil down the drain!). Serve cutlets with lemon wedges, extra Parmesan, and extra olive oil for drizzling.

How to Bread Chicken Cutlets

1. Working with 1 cutlet at a time, use tongs to dredge both sides of cutlet in flour and then dip in egg, letting excess drip back into dish.

2. Coat cutlet on both sides with bread crumb mixture. Don't press crumbs onto chicken or they'll be less crispy after they cook!

advanced

Chicken with Mushroom Sauce

I remember a time when I was very little and we went to a small underground restaurant in France. They had chicken in a mushroom sauce, like a little creamy blanket over the chicken. It was so good I couldn't even believe that it existed. Since then, I've always wanted to recreate the dish. This is the closest we've gotten (and it's really close!). You can use ¼ cup water with a squeeze of lemon juice instead of the white wine, if you prefer. This is great served with potatoes, rice, or noodles.

Prepare Ingredients

4   (3- to 4-ounce) chicken cutlets, ½ inch thick

½   teaspoon kosher salt

¼   teaspoon pepper

4   slices prosciutto

1   tablespoon extra-virgin olive oil

2   shallots, peeled and chopped fine (see page 17)

1   garlic clove, peeled and minced (see page 17)

6   ounces shiitake, button, or cremini mushrooms, trimmed and sliced

¼   cup white wine (see note, below left)

¾   cup chicken broth

¼   cup heavy cream

2   tablespoons unsalted butter, cut into ½-inch pieces and chilled

2   tablespoons chopped fresh parsley (see page 17)

Gather Cooking Equipment

▷   Large plate

▷   Paper towels

▷   12-inch skillet

▷   Tongs

▷   Serving platter

▷   Aluminum foil

▷   Wooden spoon

Start Cooking!

1. Place chicken cutlets on large plate. Pat chicken dry with paper towels. Sprinkle salt and pepper evenly over both sides of chicken.

2. Wrap 1 slice of prosciutto around center of each chicken cutlet, like a belt. Wash your hands.

3. In 12-inch skillet, heat oil over medium heat until shimmering, about 2 minutes (oil should be hot but not smoking; see page 18). Use tongs to carefully add 2 chicken cutlets to skillet, gripping around prosciutto "belt" to keep it in place. Cook until golden brown on first side, 3 to 4 minutes.

4. Use tongs to carefully flip chicken, gripping prosciutto "belt." Cook until golden brown on second side and cooked through, 2 to 4 minutes.

5. Transfer cutlets to serving platter and cover with aluminum foil. Repeat cooking with remaining 2 cutlets, transfer cutlets to serving platter, and re-cover with foil. (If skillet starts to smoke, turn heat down.)

6. Add shallots and garlic to now-empty skillet. Cook, stirring often with wooden spoon, until shallots are softened, 1 to 2 minutes. Stir in mushrooms and cook until well browned, about 4 minutes.

7. Add wine and cook, scraping bottom of skillet with wooden spoon, until liquid is evaporated, 1 to 2 minutes. Stir in broth and cream. Cook until mixture is reduced by half, about 6 minutes.

8. Turn off heat. Add chilled butter, 1 piece at a time, stirring constantly, until sauce is consistency of heavy cream. Stir in parsley and season with salt and pepper to taste (see page 15).

9. Use clean tongs to add chicken and any juices accumulated on platter to skillet. Cook over medium heat until warmed through, 1 to 2 minutes, flipping cutlets halfway through. Turn off heat.

10. Transfer chicken back to serving platter and pour sauce over top (ask an adult for help). Serve.

Chicken Tikka Masala

 I've always loved this dish, and I've eaten it maybe a billion times. We started by having it at a restaurant called Dosa Factory that was right by our school. We would go when my brother and I had half days. Since then we've tried it all over the world—London, Portugal, here in Boston . . . The sauce is satisfying, warm, and the prettiest bright orange color. Of all the versions I've tried, this recipe is my all-time favorite. I love eating this with basmati rice.

SERVES 4
TOTAL TIME 1½ hours, plus 1 hour marinating time

Prepare Ingredients

CHICKEN

- ½   cup plain whole-milk yogurt
- ½   cup fresh cilantro leaves
- 1   tablespoon lemon juice, squeezed from ½ lemon
- 1   (2-inch) piece ginger, peeled and sliced (see page 18)
- 1½   teaspoons paprika
- 1   tablespoon garam masala
- 2   garlic cloves, peeled (see page 17)
- ½   teaspoon kosher salt
- 1½   pounds boneless, skinless chicken thighs, cut into 1½-inch cubes

SAUCE

- 2   tablespoons extra-virgin olive oil
- 1   small onion, peeled and chopped (see page 17)
- 4   garlic cloves, peeled and chopped (see page 17)
- 2   tablespoons garam masala
- 1   (28-ounce) can crushed tomatoes
- 1½   teaspoons kosher salt
- 1½   cups heavy cream
- 2   teaspoons packed brown sugar
  Chopped fresh cilantro leaves (see page 17)

Gather Cooking Equipment

- ▷   Blender
- ▷   Dish towel
- ▷   Rubber spatula
- ▷   Medium bowl
- ▷   Plastic wrap
- ▷   Rimmed baking sheet
- ▷   Aluminum foil
- ▷   2 cooling racks
- ▷   Tongs
- ▷   Oven mitts
- ▷   Large saucepan
- ▷   Wooden spoon
- ▷   Ladle

Start Cooking!

1. FOR THE CHICKEN: Add yogurt, cilantro, lemon juice, ginger, paprika, 1 tablespoon garam masala, 2 garlic cloves, and ½ teaspoon salt to blender jar. Place lid on top of blender and hold lid firmly in place with folded dish towel. Turn on blender and process until smooth, about 1 minute. Stop blender and remove lid.

2. Use rubber spatula to transfer yogurt mixture to medium bowl. Add chicken to bowl and stir to coat chicken in marinade. Wash your hands. Cover bowl with plastic wrap and place in refrigerator. Let chicken marinate for at least 1 hour or up to 24 hours.

3. Adjust oven rack to upper-middle position and heat oven to 450 degrees. Line rimmed baking sheet with aluminum foil and set cooling rack in baking sheet.

~ **Keep Going!**

4. When chicken is ready, use tongs to transfer chicken to cooling rack set in rimmed baking sheet. Discard any remaining marinade.

5. Place baking sheet in oven and bake until chicken is browned on edges and cooked through, about 25 minutes. Use oven mitts to remove baking sheet from oven and place on second cooling rack (ask an adult for help).

6. FOR THE SAUCE: While chicken bakes, in large saucepan, heat oil over medium-low heat until shimmering, about 2 minutes (oil should be hot but not smoking; see page 18). Add onion and chopped garlic and cook, stirring occasionally with wooden spoon, until softened, 5 to 7 minutes. Add 2 tablespoons garam masala and cook, stirring constantly, until fragrant, about 1 minute.

7. Add crushed tomatoes and 1½ teaspoons salt and cook, stirring occasionally, until mixture comes to a boil, about 5 minutes. Turn off heat and slide saucepan to cool burner. Let sauce cool for at least 5 minutes.

8. Use ladle to carefully transfer sauce to clean blender jar (ask an adult for help—mixture will be HOT). Place lid on top of blender and hold lid firmly in place with folded dish towel. Turn on blender and process until smooth, 1 to 2 minutes. Stop blender and remove lid.

9. Pour blended sauce back into large saucepan. Stir in cream and sugar, and cook over low heat for 1 minute.

10. Add chicken to sauce and stir to combine. Cook over low heat until chicken is warmed through, about 5 minutes. Turn off heat. Serve, sprinkling individual portions with chopped cilantro.

SPICE THINGS UP

There might be only two spices on this ingredient list—garam masala and paprika—but there are a whole bunch of spices in your chicken tikka masala. How? Garam masala is a mixture of several different spices ground into a fine powder. In Hindi, "garam" means "warm" or "hot" and "masala" means "spice blend." Store-bought garam masala often includes black pepper, cardamom, cinnamon, coriander, and cumin. These spices give your dish lots of flavor, but won't make it spicy!

Black Peppercorns

Cardamom

Cinnamon Sticks

Coriander Seeds

Cumin Seeds

Turkey Meatloaf

The special thing about meatloaf is that you can eat it any way you want—hot, cold, or even in a sandwich! In our family, I like it hot, and my brother Luca likes it cold. Meatloaf is like the American version of French pâté, and it's also kind of like making a burger, but you can pack more flavors into it. This was one of the first recipes my dad ever made for us kids—he made it for our toddler group and taught the other parents how to make it too. I like to think it was a good start to my cooking career. Be sure to use ground turkey, not ground turkey breast (which may also be labeled 99 percent fat-free) in this recipe.

4 ⬛ ⬛⬛

SERVES 6 to 8
TOTAL TIME 2 hours, plus cooling time

Prepare Ingredients

1	large onion, peeled and chopped (see page 17)
2	carrots, peeled and sliced ½ inch thick
3	ounces frozen spinach
2	garlic cloves, peeled (see page 17)
2	tablespoons extra-virgin olive oil
1	tablespoon paprika
1½	teaspoons kosher salt
1	teaspoon pepper
2	pounds ground turkey
¾	cup gluten-free bread crumbs
½	cup ketchup
1	large egg
2	tablespoons gluten-free tamari
1	tablespoon yellow mustard

Gather Cooking Equipment

▷ Rimmed baking sheet
▷ Parchment paper
▷ Food processor
▷ 12-inch skillet
▷ Wooden spoon
▷ Large plate
▷ Large bowl
▷ Ruler
▷ Instant-read thermometer
▷ Oven mitts
▷ Cooling rack
▷ Chef's knife

Start Cooking!

1. Adjust oven rack to lower-middle position and heat oven to 400 degrees. Line rimmed baking sheet with parchment paper.

2. Add onion, carrots, spinach, and garlic to food processor. Lock lid into place. Hold down pulse button for 1 second, then release. Repeat until vegetables are finely chopped, about ten 1-second pulses. Remove lid and carefully remove processor blade (ask an adult for help).

3. In 12-inch skillet, combine vegetable mixture, oil, paprika, salt, and pepper. Use wooden spoon to stir until well combined. Cook over medium heat, stirring occasionally, until vegetables are softened and just beginning to brown, 15 to 18 minutes. Turn off heat.

4. Transfer vegetable mixture to large plate (ask an adult for help). Let cool completely, about 15 minutes.

5. In large bowl, combine turkey, bread crumbs, ketchup, egg, tamari, mustard, and cooled vegetable mixture. Use your hands to mix until well combined.

6. Transfer turkey mixture to center of parchment-lined baking sheet. Form into loaf about 9 inches long and 5 inches wide. Wash your hands.

7. Place baking sheet in oven. Bake until meatloaf is well browned and center of loaf registers 165 degrees on instant-read thermometer (see page 18), about 1 hour.

8. Use oven mitts to remove baking sheet from oven and place on cooling rack (ask an adult for help). Let cool for 15 minutes. Cut loaf into 1-inch-thick slices and serve. (Meatloaf can also be chilled in refrigerator and served cold.)

Steak au Poivre

I have never met a steak I didn't like. However, creamy, peppery steak au poivre became my favorite once I tried it in bistros and restaurants in Paris. Now my dad makes it at home for important occasions— holidays or birthdays or other moments that deserve something special. This recipe starts the steak in a cold pan, which makes it a little less scary to cook! I love eating this with french fries, mashed potatoes, or roasted potatoes.

Prepare Ingredients

2	tablespoons whole black peppercorns
2	(12-ounce) boneless New York strip steaks, 1½ inches thick
¾	cup beef broth
¼	cup heavy cream
¾	teaspoon kosher salt
2	tablespoons unsalted butter, cut into ½-inch pieces and chilled

Gather Cooking Equipment

▷ Heavy-duty zipper-lock plastic bag

▷ Rolling pin

▷ Large plate

▷ Paper towels

▷ 12-inch nonstick skillet

▷ Tongs

▷ Instant-read thermometer

▷ Wooden spoon

▷ Cutting board

▷ Chef's knife

▷ Serving plates

▷ Spoon

Start Cooking!

1. Place peppercorns in heavy-duty zipper-lock plastic bag and seal bag, pressing out as much air as possible. Use rolling pin to crush peppercorns (see photo, below).

2. Place steaks on large plate. Pat steaks dry with paper towels. Sprinkle half of peppercorns evenly over both sides of steaks.

3. Place steaks 1 inch apart in 12-inch nonstick skillet. Wash your hands. Turn heat to high and cook steaks for 2 minutes. Use tongs to flip steaks and cook on second side for 2 minutes.

4. Reduce heat to medium. Flip steaks and continue to cook, flipping every 2 minutes, until well browned and meat registers 120 to 125 degrees on instant-read thermometer (see page 18), 4 to 10 minutes. (Steaks should be sizzling gently in skillet; if not, increase heat slightly. If skillet starts to smoke, turn heat down.)

Keep Going!

How to Crush Peppercorns

Place peppercorns in heavy-duty zipper-lock plastic bag and seal bag, pressing out as much air as possible. Use rolling pin to crush peppercorns. Make sure every peppercorn is cracked open—you do not want any whole peppercorns!

5. Transfer steaks to clean large plate. Add remaining cracked peppercorns to skillet and cook for 30 seconds. Use wooden spoon to stir in broth. Bring to a simmer (small bubbles should break often across surface of mixture). Cook until reduced by half, 3 to 4 minutes.

6. Stir in cream and salt and cook for 2 minutes. Turn off heat. Add chilled butter, 1 piece at a time, stirring constantly, until sauce is consistency of heavy cream.

7. Transfer steaks to cutting board. Use chef's knife to cut each steak in half crosswise (the short way). Pour steak juices remaining on plate into skillet and stir to combine.

8. Transfer steaks back to skillet. Use tongs to flip steaks in sauce until well coated, about 1 minute.

9. Transfer steaks to serving plates. Serve with extra sauce spooned over top.

Cold-Start Steak

I've seen you cook a lot of steaks, and usually you add them to a really hot pan—I always hear the sizzle! Why are we adding these steaks to a cold skillet?

Great observation, Verveine. It's a much safer and easier cooking technique, but it still gives you perfectly cooked steak.

How does it work?

It lets the steaks heat up gradually, so they're less likely to overcook. And flipping the steaks every 2 minutes helps them cook evenly. It gives each side a break from the hot skillet.

And it's way less smoky too.

Exactly. Using a nonstick skillet means you don't have to add any oil to the pan, so there's less smoky, splattery mess, but you still end up with a perfectly browned steak.

Beef Kofte

This is a Middle Eastern dish made with ground meat and lots of spices. It has a perfect balance of seasoning and flavor. My dad and Luca love to eat kofte with yogurt sauce (plain yogurt, a squeeze of lemon juice, and a pinch of salt), but I prefer them with a drizzle of extra-virgin olive oil, a squeeze of lemon, and a sprinkle of chopped cilantro or parsley.

SERVES 4 (Makes 10 kofte)
TOTAL TIME 1 hour

Prepare Ingredients

1 onion, peeled and chopped (see page 17)

½ cup fresh cilantro leaves, plus extra chopped fresh cilantro or parsley for serving (see page 17)

1 pound 85 percent lean ground beef

1 teaspoon kosher salt

1 teaspoon ground cumin

½ teaspoon curry powder

½ teaspoon paprika

½ teaspoon ground cinnamon

½ teaspoon ground coriander

¼ teaspoon pepper

1 teaspoon extra-virgin olive oil, plus extra for drizzling

Lemon wedges

Gather Cooking Equipment

▷ Food processor

▷ Rubber spatula

▷ Large bowl

▷ Rimmed baking sheet

▷ Parchment paper

▷ Ruler

▷ 12-inch cast-iron skillet or 12-inch nonstick skillet

▷ Tongs

▷ Instant-read thermometer

▷ Serving platter

Start Cooking!

1. Add onion and cilantro to food processor. Lock lid into place. Hold down pulse button for 1 second, then release. Repeat pulsing until mixture is finely chopped, about ten 1-second pulses.

2. Remove lid and carefully remove processor blade (ask an adult for help). Use rubber spatula to transfer onion mixture to large bowl.

3. Carefully replace processor blade (ask an adult for help). Add beef, salt, cumin, curry powder, paprika, cinnamon, coriander, and pepper to processor bowl. Lock lid back into place. Hold down pulse button for 1 second, then release. Repeat pulsing until mixture is well combined and looks sticky, ten to fifteen 1-second pulses.

4. Remove lid and carefully remove processor blade (ask an adult for help). Use rubber spatula to transfer beef mixture to bowl with onion mixture. Stir until well combined.

5. Line rimmed baking sheet with parchment paper. Lightly wet your hands. Divide mixture into 10 equal portions. Shape 10 kofte following photo, below, and place on parchment-lined baking sheet.

6. In 12-inch cast-iron skillet, heat oil over medium heat until shimmering, about 3 minutes (oil should be hot but not smoking; see page 18). Use tongs to carefully place kofte in skillet. Cook until browned on first side, about 5 minutes.

7. Use tongs to carefully flip kofte and cook until browned on second side and center of meat registers 160 degrees on instant-read thermometer (see page 18), 5 to 7 minutes. Turn off heat.

8. Transfer kofte to serving platter. Drizzle with extra oil, sprinkle with chopped cilantro, and serve with lemon wedges.

How to Shape Kofte

Shape each portion of meat mixture into oval shape about 3½ inches long and 1¼ inches thick. Place on parchment-lined baking sheet.

Beef Bourguignon

What makes beef bourguignon so special is that it melts in your mouth and it's covered in one of the best sauces ever. It's rich and meaty and thick. People don't often think of this dish as the perfect pasta sauce, but it's one of my favorites, thanks to a restaurant in Paris that we often went to called Chez Joséphine. They served it with elbow macaroni and tiny carrot pieces. Go make Fresh Pasta (page 70), Spinach Orecchiette (page 74), or Potato Gnocchi (page 80) to eat with this dish—you won't regret it! You can use 3 cups of canned tomato puree instead of the red wine, if you prefer, but your stew will have a more tomato sauce-y flavor than traditional beef bourguignon.

SERVES 6 to 8
TOTAL TIME 1 hour, plus 3 to 4 hours hands-off cooking time

Prepare Ingredients

3   pounds boneless beef short ribs or chuck flap, cut into 2-inch cubes

1   teaspoon kosher salt

½   teaspoon pepper

2   tablespoons extra-virgin olive oil

2   slices bacon, cut into small pieces

3   carrots, washed, trimmed, and cut into 2-inch chunks

2   onions, peeled and chopped (see page 17)

3   tablespoons tomato paste

2   garlic cloves, peeled and chopped (see page 17)

3   cups red wine (see note, below left)

3   cups beef broth

1   tablespoon gluten-free tamari

2   sprigs fresh thyme

2   bay leaves

¼   cup water

2   tablespoons cornstarch

Gather Cooking Equipment

▷   Large plate
▷   Paper towels
▷   Dutch oven with lid
▷   Wooden spoon
▷   Slotted spoon
▷   Tongs
▷   2 bowls (1 medium, 1 small)
▷   Fork
▷   Oven mitts
▷   Spoon

Start Cooking!

1. Adjust oven rack to lower-middle position and heat oven to 325 degrees. Line large plate with double layer of paper towels and place next to stovetop.

2. Pat beef dry with more paper towels. Sprinkle salt and pepper evenly over all sides of beef. Wash your hands.

3. In Dutch oven, heat oil over medium heat until shimmering, about 2 minutes (oil should be hot but not smoking; see page 18). Add bacon and cook, stirring occasionally with wooden spoon, until browned, about 5 minutes. Turn off heat. Use slotted spoon to transfer bacon to paper towel–lined plate.

4. Increase heat to medium-high. Carefully add half of beef to now-empty pot. Cook until well browned on first side, 2 to 4 minutes. Use tongs to flip beef and cook until well browned on second side, 2 to 4 minutes. Transfer beef to medium bowl. Repeat browning with remaining beef, and transfer to bowl.

5. Reduce heat to medium. Add carrots and onions to now-empty pot and cook, stirring often with wooden spoon, until lightly browned, about 5 minutes.

6. Add tomato paste and garlic and cook for 1 minute. Stir in wine, broth, tamari, thyme sprigs, and bay leaves, scraping bottom of pot with wooden spoon. Carefully add browned beef and bacon. Bring mixture to simmer (small bubbles should break often across surface of mixture). Turn off heat. Cover pot with lid.

7. Ask an adult to place pot in oven. Cook until beef is fork-tender and falling apart, 3 to 4 hours.

8. Ask an adult to use oven mitts to remove pot from oven, place on stovetop, and carefully remove lid. Place oven mitts on handles so you remember that pot is VERY HOT. Use tongs to remove and discard bay leaves and thyme sprigs.

9. In small bowl, use spoon to stir together water and cornstarch. Stir cornstarch mixture into pot and bring to a boil over medium-high heat. Reduce heat to medium and cook until sauce has thickened to consistency of heavy cream, 6 to 8 minutes. Turn off heat.

10. Season with salt and pepper to taste (see page 15). Serve.

Vietnamese-Style Meatballs

These delicious little meatballs are inspired by Vietnamese bún chá, which is served with lettuce, vermicelli, and herbs. We like to eat these meatballs in lettuce leaves with a sprinkle of mint and a squeeze of lime. What makes these meatballs different from traditional Italian meatballs are that they are lighter, smaller, and PACKED with umami (see page 14). Look for fried shallots in the international section of your grocery store or in East or Southeast Asian markets. If you can't find them, you can leave them out.

SERVES 4 (Makes 16 meatballs)
TOTAL TIME 50 minutes

Prepare Ingredients

1   small onion, peeled and chopped (see page 17)

3   scallions, root ends trimmed and scallions chopped

¼   cup fresh cilantro leaves

1   pound ground pork

¼   cup gluten-free fried shallots, chopped (see note, below left)

1   tablespoon gluten-free tamari

1   teaspoon kosher salt

1   teaspoon pepper

1   teaspoon sugar

½   teaspoon fish sauce

2   tablespoons vegetable oil

    Bibb lettuce leaves

    Chopped fresh mint (see page 17)

    Lime wedges

Gather Cooking Equipment

▷ Rimmed baking sheet
▷ Aluminum foil
▷ Food processor
▷ Rubber spatula
▷ Large bowl
▷ Oven mitts
▷ Cooling rack
▷ Tongs
▷ Serving platter

Start Cooking!

1. Adjust oven rack to upper-middle position and heat oven to 475 degrees. Line rimmed baking sheet with aluminum foil.

2. Add onion, scallions, and cilantro to food processor. Lock lid into place. Hold down pulse button for 1 second, then release. Repeat pulsing until vegetables are finely chopped, about ten 1-second pulses.

3. Remove lid and carefully remove processor blade (ask an adult for help). Use rubber spatula to transfer vegetable mixture to large bowl. Add pork, fried shallots, tamari, salt, pepper, sugar, and fish sauce to bowl. Use your hands to mix until well combined.

4. Divide mixture into 16 equal portions. Roll each portion into ball, and place on foil-lined baking sheet. Wash your hands.

5. Drizzle oil evenly over meatballs. Place baking sheet in oven. Bake until well browned, 15 to 20 minutes.

6. Use oven mitts to remove baking sheet from oven and place on cooling rack (ask an adult for help). Use tongs to transfer meatballs to serving platter. Serve with Bibb lettuce, mint, and lime wedges.

A WORLD OF MEATBALLS

In the United States, Italian-inspired meatballs coated in tomato sauce tend to get all the glory. But meatballs are a part of cuisines around the globe, made with different ground meats and served in different ways. This recipe is inspired by the grilled meatballs served as part of Vietnamese bún chả.

VIETNAM
Bún Chả

JAPAN
Tsukune

SPAIN + LATIN AMERICA
Albóndigas

SWEDEN
Köttbullar

CHINA
Shīzi Tóu

Teriyaki "Hibachi" Salmon

The first time I had this salmon recipe was only a year ago at a friend's house. It's different from all the other ways I've tried salmon. I loved it and so did my brother. He loved it so much that it's the only salmon he'll eat now! This salmon gets a caramelized top from the broiler, and it's a little sweet from the honey. Sake is a kind of Japanese alcohol made from rice; you can leave it out, if you prefer. I love to eat this salmon with steamed white rice and nori sheets—you can make little "tacos" by wrapping some rice and salmon in the nori!

SERVES 4
TOTAL TIME 40 minutes, plus 1 hour marinating time

Prepare Ingredients

¼   cup gluten-free tamari

1½ tablespoons mirin

1   tablespoon lemon juice, squeezed from ½ lemon

2   teaspoons honey

1   teaspoon toasted sesame oil

1   tablespoon grated fresh ginger (see page 18)

2   garlic cloves, peeled and minced (see page 17)

2   teaspoons sake (optional)

4   (6-ounce) skinless salmon fillets

1   tablespoon toasted sesame seeds

2   scallions, dark-green parts only, sliced thin

Gather Cooking Equipment

▷ 2 bowls (1 medium, 1 small)

▷ Whisk

▷ 1-tablespoon measuring spoon

▷ Plastic wrap

▷ Rimmed baking sheet

▷ Aluminum foil

▷ 2 cooling racks

▷ Instant-read thermometer

▷ Oven mitts

▷ Pastry brush

▷ Spatula

▷ Serving plates

Start Cooking!

1. In medium bowl, whisk together tamari, mirin, lemon juice, honey, oil, ginger, garlic, and sake (if using). Measure 2 tablespoons tamari mixture into small bowl and reserve for brushing in step 6.

2. Add salmon to bowl with remaining tamari mixture and turn to coat salmon. Wash your hands. Cover bowl with plastic wrap. Place in refrigerator to marinate for at least 1 hour or up to 24 hours (the longer the better!).

3. Adjust oven rack to upper-middle position and heat broiler. Line rimmed baking sheet with aluminum foil and set cooling rack in baking sheet.

4. When fish is ready, remove bowl from refrigerator and discard plastic wrap. Place salmon fillets on cooling rack set in rimmed baking sheet. Discard remaining marinade in bowl. Wash your hands.

5. Place baking sheet in oven and broil until salmon registers 125 degrees on instant-read thermometer (see page 18), 6 to 8 minutes.

6. Ask an adult to use oven mitts to remove baking sheet from oven and place on second cooling rack. Use pastry brush to carefully brush salmon with reserved 2 tablespoons tamari mixture (be careful—baking sheet will be HOT).

7. Use spatula to transfer salmon to serving plates. Sprinkle salmon with sesame seeds and scallions. Serve.

From Chef Ken: From Hawaii via Japan

Today, English speakers use the word "hibachi" to refer to small charcoal or wood-burning grills with metal or cast-iron cooking grates (in Japan, these are known as "shichirin"). Japanese immigrants brought this cooking tool to Hawaii and it took off, with hibachi restaurants popping up all over the islands and people using these little grills at home. When I'd take trips to Hawaii, I'd cook on a hibachi all the time—it's perfect for kids learning to grill, and I loved to cook salmon on it. But since you might not have a hibachi at home, I created this recipe that uses the broiler instead. The superhot broiler causes the sugars in the marinade to brown and char, mimicking the flavor of the hibachi grill.

Salt-Crusted Branzino

Ever since I was little, we've gone to my dad's restaurant Toro and ordered the whole branzino, which comes out covered in a salt crust, making it look like a mummy. (My brother and I used to eat the eyeballs straight out of the fish. They're good!) Every time I've eaten this dish, the same thing happens—family, friends, or people I was just getting to know would share the fish, with everyone eating it in their own way. It brings people together at the dinner table. You can use whole snapper instead of branzino, if you prefer.

Prepare Ingredients

2   (1- to 1½-pound)
    whole branzino

⅛   teaspoon pepper

¼   teaspoon plus 5 cups kosher salt,
    measured separately

2   sprigs fresh parsley

2   sprigs fresh thyme

2   sprigs fresh rosemary

2   lemon slices, plus lemon wedges
    for serving

3   large egg whites (see page 16)

2   tablespoons extra-virgin olive
    oil, plus extra for serving

Gather Cooking Equipment

▷   2 rimmed baking sheets

▷   Parchment paper

▷   Paper towels

▷   Large bowl

▷   Whisk

▷   Wooden spoon

▷   Ruler

▷   Oven mitts

▷   Cooling rack

▷   Serving spoon

▷   Fish spatula

▷   Serving plates

Start Cooking!

1. Adjust oven rack to middle position and heat oven to 400 degrees. Line rimmed baking sheet with parchment paper and set aside. Line second rimmed baking sheet with paper towels.

2. Rinse inside cavities of fish in sink under cold running water. Place on paper towel–lined baking sheet. Pat fish dry with more paper towels.

3. Sprinkle inside cavities of fish with pepper and ¼ teaspoon salt. Place 1 parsley sprig, 1 thyme sprig, 1 rosemary sprig, and 1 lemon slice inside cavity of each fish. Wash your hands.

4. In large bowl, whisk egg whites until frothy, about 30 seconds. Add remaining 5 cups salt to egg whites and stir with wooden spoon until well combined and mixture looks like wet sand.

5. Pack fish in salt mixture and drizzle with oil following photos, below. Wash your hands.

6. Place baking sheet in oven. Bake until salt crust is lightly browned, about 30 minutes.

Keep Going!

How to Make a Salt Crust

1. Divide half of salt mixture into 2 even mounds on parchment-lined baking sheet. Pat mounds into 5-by-14-inch rectangles, spaced about 1 inch apart.

2. Lay 1 fish lengthwise across each mound. Drizzle both fish evenly with oil. Gently pack remaining salt mixture over each fish, covering each fish completely (it should look like a fish mummy!).

7. Use oven mitts to remove baking sheet from oven and place on cooling rack (ask an adult for help).

8. Use back of serving spoon to gently tap top and sides of salt crusts, cracking them into large pieces. Discard salt crusts, brushing any remaining salt off skin (ask an adult for help—baking sheet will be HOT).

9. Ask an adult to fillet each branzino and transfer to serving plates following photos, right. Carefully inspect fillets for any extra bones and discard if you find them. Drizzle with extra oil and serve with lemon wedges.

From Chef Ken: Get Salty

This is one of my favorite techniques for cooking whole fish. It's pretty simple, but it looks really impressive and gives you perfectly cooked (and perfectly seasoned) fish every time. The thick layer of salt forms a barrier between the fish and the oven's heat, so the fish cooks slowly and evenly. The salt also traps steam, meaning that the fish stays moist and juicy—there's no way you'll end up with dry fish when you're using this method. Finally, since we're using 5 cups of salt in this recipe, you might be worried that your fish will turn out really salty. Don't be! Only a tiny bit of salt actually makes its way into the fish, giving it just the right amount of seasoning.

How to Fillet a Fish

1. Use tip of overturned serving spoon to cut through skin behind head, along gills.

2. Turn spoon right side up and continue gently cutting through skin along spine from head to tail. Gently peel away skin and discard.

3. Use fish spatula to cut exposed fillet in half crosswise (the short way), then gently slide spatula between fillet and bones to separate; transfer fillets to serving plates.

4. Gently peel spine away from bottom fillet and discard. Use spoon to loosen skin around edges of bottom fillet. Use spatula to cut fillet in half crosswise, then gently slide spatula underneath fillets and transfer to serving plates, leaving skin behind. Discard skin and bones. Repeat with remaining fish.

Crunchy Halibut with Orange-Ginger Sauce

This is my favorite fish dish. The halibut isn't too fishy; it almost tastes like chicken but not as meaty. It's a good fish dish even if you don't love fish. (My brother Luca approves!) It's breaded on the top, which makes it really crunchy. You can substitute cod for the halibut in this recipe, if you prefer. For information on substituting gluten-free flours, see page 12.

4 🔲🔲 **SERVES 4**
TOTAL TIME 1 hour

Prepare Ingredients

ORANGE-GINGER SAUCE

2	cups (16 ounces) orange juice
¼	cup honey
1	tablespoon grated fresh ginger (see page 18)
1½	teaspoons gluten-free tamari
½	teaspoon hot sauce
2	tablespoons chopped fresh cilantro (see page 17)

FISH

½	cup (2½ ounces) Cup4Cup Gluten-Free Multipurpose Flour
2	large eggs
1	cup gluten-free panko bread crumbs
1	teaspoon grated lemon zest, zested from ½ lemon
1	teaspoon chopped fresh cilantro (see page 17)
4	(6-ounce) skinless halibut fillets, 1 to 1½ inches thick
½	teaspoon kosher salt
¼	teaspoon pepper
¼	cup extra-virgin olive oil

Gather Cooking Equipment

▷ Small saucepan with lid
▷ 3 shallow dishes
▷ Fork
▷ Paper towels
▷ Large plate

▷ 12-inch nonstick skillet
▷ Tongs
▷ Instant-read thermometer
▷ Serving plates
▷ Spoon

Start Cooking!

1. FOR THE ORANGE-GINGER SAUCE: In small saucepan, combine orange juice, honey, ginger, tamari, and hot sauce. Bring mixture to a boil over medium-high heat. Reduce heat to medium and continue cooking at low boil until sauce has syrupy consistency, 25 to 30 minutes.

2. Turn off heat and slide saucepan to cool burner. Stir in 2 tablespoons cilantro and season with salt to taste (see page 15). Cover saucepan with lid to keep warm.

3. FOR THE FISH: Spread flour in shallow dish. Place eggs in second shallow dish and beat with fork until well combined. In third shallow dish, toss panko, lemon zest, and 1 teaspoon cilantro until well combined.

4. Use paper towels to pat fish dry. Sprinkle salt and pepper evenly over both sides of fish.

5. Working with 1 piece of fish at a time, dip top side of fish in flour, then dip into egg, letting excess drip back into dish. Dip top side of fish in bread crumbs, pressing firmly on crumbs to adhere. Place on large plate. Wash your hands.

6. In 12-inch nonstick skillet, heat oil over medium heat until shimmering, about 2 minutes (oil should be hot but not smoking; see page 18). Carefully place fish in skillet, breaded side down (ask an adult for help). Cook until golden brown on first side, 4 to 6 minutes.

7. Use tongs to carefully flip fillets. Cook until fish registers 135 to 140 degrees on instant-read thermometer (see page 18), 5 to 10 minutes. Turn off heat.

8. Use tongs to transfer fish to serving plates. Use spoon to drizzle sauce around fish (not on top!). Serve.

Chapter 5

My Dad, the Chef

Maki

When I was little, we would take class trips to Uni, one of my dad's restaurants that's known for its sushi. We'd get to make our own maki (sushi rolls), and they would have all of these different options for fillings: salmon, tuna, avocado . . . even marshmallows and chocolate, though I wouldn't recommend those! Learning to roll maki can take a little bit of practice, but in a few tries you'll get the hang of it. And even if your maki don't look perfect, they'll still taste great! Freshness is key when serving raw fish. Talk to your fishmonger to make sure you are purchasing fresh, high-quality, sushi-grade fish. We love thick, tangy Kewpie mayo in our maki, but you can use regular mayonnaise, if desired.

4 ⊞ SERVES 4 (Makes 8 rolls)
TOTAL TIME 2 hours

Prepare Ingredients

RICE

 3 cups sushi rice

3⅓ cups water

 7 tablespoons seasoned rice vinegar

 ⅓ cup (2⅓ ounces) sugar

 2 tablespoons kosher salt

 1 tablespoon red wine vinegar

1½ teaspoons mirin

FILLING

 1 English cucumber and/or 1 ripe avocado and/or 1 (8-ounce) sushi-grade boneless, skinless salmon or tuna fillet

 ½ cup Kewpie mayonnaise (optional)

2–3 teaspoons sriracha (optional)

 1 tablespoon lemon juice, squeezed from ½ lemon (optional)

 8 (8-by-7½-inch) sheets nori

   Gluten-free tamari

Gather Cooking Equipment

▷ Fine-mesh strainer

▷ 3 bowls (1 large, 1 medium, 1 small)

▷ Large saucepan with lid

▷ Rubber spatula

▷ Whisk

▷ Oven mitts

▷ Dish towel

▷ Cutting board

▷ Chef's knife

▷ Spoon

▷ Sushi mat or 10-inch square piece of parchment paper

▷ 1-cup dry measuring cup

▷ Ruler

▷ 1-teaspoon measuring spoon

Start Cooking!

1. FOR THE RICE: Set fine-mesh strainer over large bowl and set in sink. Place rice in strainer. Rinse rice under cold running water, emptying bowl as it fills, until water in bowl is clear, 5 to 7 rinses. Shake strainer to drain rice well. Discard water in bowl.

2. Transfer rice to large saucepan. Use rubber spatula to stir in 3⅓ cups water. Bring rice to a boil over medium-high heat. Reduce heat to low, cover saucepan with lid, and cook for 20 minutes.

3. Turn off heat and slide saucepan to cool burner. Let rice sit, covered, for 10 minutes to finish cooking.

4. While rice cooks, in medium bowl, whisk rice vinegar, sugar, salt, red wine vinegar, and mirin until sugar and salt are dissolved.

Keep Going!

5. When rice is ready, use oven mitts to remove lid from saucepan. Use rubber spatula to transfer cooked rice to clean, dry large bowl (ask an adult for help).

6. Pour half of vinegar mixture over rice and gently stir until absorbed. Add remaining vinegar mixture and stir again until absorbed. Cover bowl with dish towel and let rice cool for 20 minutes.

7. FOR THE FILLING: While rice is cooling, if using cucumber, place cucumber on cutting board and use chef's knife to trim ends. Discard ends. Cut cucumber in half crosswise (the short way). Then cut each half lengthwise (the long way). Lay cucumber halves flat side down on cutting board and cut into quarters lengthwise. (You should have 16 spears total.)

8. If using avocado, cut avocado in half lengthwise around pit. Using your hands, twist both halves in opposite directions to separate. Use spoon to scoop out pit. Discard pit. Scoop out avocado from skin. Discard skins. Lay avocado halves flat side down on cutting board and cut into thin slices.

9. If using fish, cut salmon or tuna lengthwise (the long way) into 4 pieces. Lay each piece flat on cutting board. Cut each piece lengthwise again into 4 strips. (You should have 16 pieces total.)

10. If you want to add spicy mayo to your maki filling, in small bowl, use spoon to stir together mayonnaise, sriracha, and lemon juice.

11. Fill and shape maki following photos, right. Transfer finished roll, seam side down, to clean cutting board. Repeat filling and shaping with remaining nori sheets, rice, fish, cucumber and/or avocado, and spicy mayo (if using).

12. Cut each roll crosswise into 6 or 8 equal pieces, dipping knife in water between cuts if it gets sticky (ask an adult for help). Serve with tamari and extra spicy mayo (if using) for dipping.

Secrets of Sushi Rice

When most people think of maki, they focus on the fillings. But if you don't get the rice right, your sushi won't be nearly as good.

Great sushi rice has the best texture—it's slightly sticky, soft but a little chewy, and it's never mushy.

Rinsing your rice is the secret to that texture. It gets rid of some of the starch on the outside of the rice. If you didn't rinse, that starch would turn mushy and gummy when the rice cooks.

That makes sense . . . I also love that it tastes more complex than just plain rice. The sugar, salt, vinegars, and mirin give it a salty-tangy-sweet flavor.

Yeah, getting the balance just right is key. I think we nailed it here.

How to Shape Maki

One of the best parts of making maki is that you get to choose your fillings! You can use any combination of fish, cucumber, and/or avocado that you like.

1. Place 1 nori sheet, shiny side down, on sushi mat, with longer side parallel to bottom edge of mat.

2. Use your lightly wet hands to scoop about 1 cup cooled rice and form into baseball shape. Place rice ball on nori and spread rice into even layer, all the way to edges except for 1-inch border at top.

3. Place 2 strips of fish in line across middle of rice. Add 2 cucumber spears and/or 2 to 3 avocado slices on top, overlapping ends slightly if needed. Drizzle 1 to 2 teaspoons spicy mayo mixture over top (if using).

4. Use sushi mat to lift and roll bottom edge of nori sheet up and over filling.

5. Gently squeeze and pull mat towards you to tighten.

6. Lift up edge of mat and continue to roll remaining nori and rice into log. Use mat to gently squeeze outside to seal and tighten.

Oysters with Strawberry Mignonette

Oysters bring the ocean right into your kitchen. When you open an oyster and smell it, it smells just like you're swimming in the ocean. If you've never tried one, I highly recommend taking a taste. They might look kind of weird, but I think they are absolutely delicious, especially with this strawberry mignonette—a tangy sauce that tastes very lightly of strawberries and perfectly complements the briny, oceany flavor of the oysters. We love oysters from Island Creek Oysters in Duxbury, Massachusetts. The great news is that they can ship you fresh oysters, wherever you live! As you're shucking your oysters, if one doesn't have any liquid inside it or it smells funky, throw it out.

Prepare Ingredients

STRAWBERRY MIGNONETTE

3   strawberries, hulled and cut into ¼-inch pieces (see photo, below right)

1   small shallot, peeled and minced (see page 17)

2   tablespoons seasoned rice vinegar

2   tablespoons white wine vinegar

⅛   teaspoon kosher salt

⅛   teaspoon pepper

OYSTERS
     Crushed ice

12 oysters (see note, below left, about shopping for oysters)

Gather Cooking Equipment

▷   Small serving bowl

▷   Spoon

▷   Plastic wrap

▷   Large, deep serving platter

▷   Stiff-bristled brush

▷   Dish towel

▷   Oyster knife

Start Cooking!

1. FOR THE STRAWBERRY MIGNONETTE: In small serving bowl, use spoon to stir together all strawberry mignonette ingredients. Cover bowl with plastic wrap and place in refrigerator for at least 1 hour or up to 4 days.

2. FOR THE OYSTERS: Fill large, deep serving platter with crushed ice. Rinse oysters in sink under cold running water, scrubbing well with stiff-bristled brush.

3. Ask an adult to help you shuck oysters following photos, pages 168–169. Place oysters in half shells on ice, being careful not to spill liquid in shells (this is the delicious oyster brine!).

4. Spoon a little strawberry mignonette over each oyster. Serve immediately, slurping oysters from shells!

Keep Going!

How to Hull Strawberries

Use paring knife to slice strawberries in half lengthwise (the long way) through stem end. Place strawberries flat side down. Use tip of knife to cut out green leafy part.

From Chef Ken: The World Is Your Oyster

Oysters are amazing, with their tender meat and salty brine. Here's a fascinating fact about these edible bivalves: Depending on the exact location of the water where they're grown and harvested, the same species of oyster can have very different flavors. Though, in general, oysters grown in the Atlantic ocean taste saltier than the ones grown in the Pacific ocean, which taste slightly sweeter. There are lots of ways to eat raw oysters: plain, with a squeeze of lemon, with a dash of hot sauce, or with a spoonful of mignonette. My favorite? It depends on my mood, but I've never met an oyster I didn't like.

How to Shuck Oysters

Shucking oysters is tricky and can be dangerous—ask an adult to teach you how to do these steps. Always use an oyster knife when shucking oysters, using any other type of knife is too dangerous and won't work well.

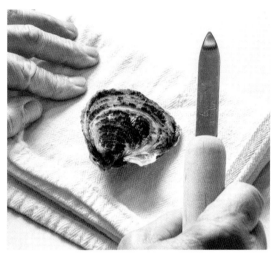

1. Fold dish towel in half. Working with 1 oyster at a time, lay oyster on top of dish towel, flat side up, with hinge (the narrow end) facing you.

2. Fold towel over top of oyster, keeping hinge exposed (the towel will help protect your hand from the shell and knife).

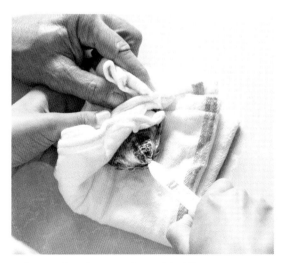

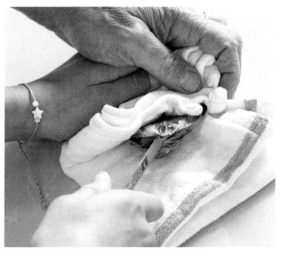

3. Set one hand on top of towel, holding oyster in place. Insert tip of oyster knife into hinge of oyster. Then work tip of oyster knife into hinge with twisting and rocking motion to pop open shell.

4. Once hinge is popped, turn knife 90 degrees away from you by twisting your wrist (like you are revving a motorcycle). Wipe away any grit from tip of knife using towel under oyster.

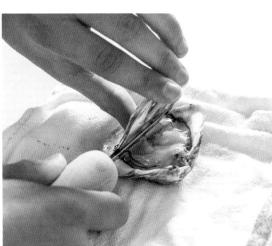

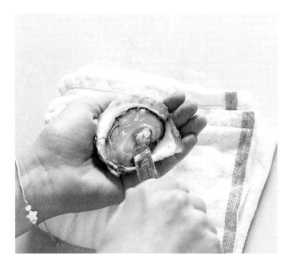

5. Work knife back into oyster, sliding it away from you and flush against top flat side of shell, severing adductor muscle that holds oyster meat in place. Remove and discard top shell.

6. Lift oyster into palm of your hand. Slide knife under bottom of oyster meat and scrape to release from bottom shell. Remove any pieces of shell with tip of knife and wipe on dish towel. Place oyster on ice on serving platter.

Fancy Tomato Water

This tastes like drinking a perfectly ripe, fresh tomato. It's so cool to see the mixture start out bright red but eventually end up almost perfectly clear. When you add the little cherry tomato and basil garnish, this feels like a fancy drink that you might enjoy on a special occasion—maybe on your birthday or New Year's Eve (see page 172)? When I want to feel extra-celebratory, I like to sip mine from one of my parents' martini glasses, but any glass you have will work. If you don't have cheesecloth, you can use a double layer of coffee filters to drain the tomatoes instead.

SERVES 4
TOTAL TIME 15 minutes, plus 8 hours chilling time

Prepare Ingredients

5   vine-ripened or plum tomatoes (1½–2 pounds)

¾   teaspoon kosher salt

2   cherry tomatoes, cut in half

4   small basil leaves

Gather Cooking Equipment

▷   Food processor

▷   Fine-mesh strainer

▷   4-cup liquid measuring cup or medium bowl with spout

▷   Cheesecloth

▷   Plastic wrap

▷   4 small, clear glasses (fancy ones, if you have them!)

▷   4 toothpicks

Start Cooking!

1. Add tomatoes and salt to food processor. Lock lid into place. Turn on processor and process until smooth, about 1 minute. Stop processor. Remove lid and carefully remove processor blade (ask an adult for help).

2. Set fine-mesh strainer over 4-cup liquid measuring cup. Line strainer with 4 layers of cheesecloth. Pour pureed tomato mixture into cheesecloth-lined strainer. Cover strainer and measuring cup with plastic wrap. Place in refrigerator and let drain for at least 8 hours or up to 24 hours.

3. Remove liquid measuring cup from refrigerator. Gather edges of cheesecloth together and gently squeeze over strainer to release any remaining liquid (don't squeeze too hard!). Discard cheesecloth and solids.

4. Divide tomato water evenly among 4 glasses (about ½ cup per glass). Slide 1 cherry tomato half and 1 basil leaf onto each toothpick. Place 1 toothpick in each glass. Serve.

From Chef Ken: (Not) Seeing Red

These crystal-clear drinks that I used to serve at my restaurant, Clio, have all the flavor of a fresh tomato, but none of the red color. It might look like kitchen magic, but it's all thanks to the science of filtration. Pureeing the tomatoes in the food processor releases their liquid (tomatoes, like many fruits and vegetables, are mostly water). Then, the four layers of cheesecloth (the filters) trap all of the red-colored particles as the tomato puree drips through them. You're left with a liquid that tastes fresher and lighter than store-bought tomato juice.

New Year's Eve Celebration

I recommend eating these two fancy dishes on a special occasion, such as New Year's Eve. I love the salty, crunchy potato chips with the caviar, which are like little salty pearls from the ocean. My dad tried to get me to eat the uni spoon for a long time. One day I decided to be brave and try it. It was the most perfect bite of food I've ever tasted—no exaggeration!

Caviar and Chips

SERVES 4

Prepare Ingredients

- ⅓   cup crème fraîche
- 1   (8½-ounce) bag Kettle brand Salt and Vinegar or Sea Salt Potato Chips
- 1   ounce caviar or roe

From Chef Ken: All About Caviar

Caviar is, essentially, fish eggs. "True" caviar is made exclusively from sturgeon eggs (sturgeon are a type of fish), while eggs from any other fish are commonly called roe. We particularly like osetra caviar, salmon roe, or trout roe, but any kind that you'd like to try will work in this recipe. Look for caviar at specialty markets, fish stores, or online—we like ordering from Caviar Russe. It's a lot of work to harvest caviar, which makes it expensive and best for serving on special occasions.

STEP 1
Dollop small amount of crème fraîche onto 1 potato chip.

STEP 2
Top with smaller scoop of caviar.

STEP 3
Eat in one bite!

Uni Spoons

SERVES 4

Prepare Ingredients

12	pieces (tongues) uni
4	drops gluten-free tamari
4	drops lemon juice, squeezed from ½ lemon
2	teaspoons caviar
4	quail egg yolks (see page 16)
	Flake sea salt

STEP 1
Place 3 pieces uni on each spoon.

STEP 2
Use tiny spoon to add 1 drop tamari and 1 drop lemon juice on top of uni in each spoon.

STEP 3
Add ½ teaspoon caviar to each spoon in mound on top of uni.

STEP 4
Add 1 quail egg yolk to each spoon next to caviar.

STEP 5
Sprinkle pinch flake sea salt over each egg yolk.

STEP 6
Serve immediately, making sure to eat the entire spoon together in one bite!

From Chef Ken: Two Special Ingredients

Uni is the small bit of edible meat found inside a sea urchin. Since it's eaten raw, it's important that the uni you buy is very fresh. Find it at a fishmonger that also sells sushi-grade fish or at an Asian specialty market. Because sea urchins are caught in the wild, uni can be very expensive, so this is a dish to splurge on for a special occasion. Look for small, speckled quail eggs in specialty markets.

Pasta al Tartufo Nero di Norcia

A few years ago, our family went on a trip to Norcia, Italy, and we got to go truffle hunting (truffles are a special kind of mushroom that grows underground). We walked through the woods with a cute curly-haired dog and its owner. When the dog smelled a truffle, it would start digging to show the owner where it was. After we finished, I remember trying this pasta with truffle sauce and being amazed by the flavor! We developed this recipe with Melchiorri Tartufata Black Truffle Sauce, which is actually a paste. You can find it at specialty Italian markets or online. We love penne in this recipe, but you can substitute 12 ounces of any short pasta shape. For information on our favorite gluten-free pasta, see page 12.

Prepare Ingredients

2	tablespoons black truffle paste
1	anchovy fillet
1	garlic clove, peeled and chopped (see page 17)
¼	cup plus 4 quarts water, measured separately
3	tablespoons extra-virgin olive oil
2	tablespoons kosher salt
12	ounces gluten-free penne pasta
3	tablespoons unsalted butter, cut into 6 pieces and chilled
	Grated Parmesan cheese

Gather Cooking Equipment

▷ Food processor

▷ Rubber spatula

▷ 11-inch sauté pan or 12-inch skillet

▷ Large pot

▷ Wooden spoon

▷ Ladle

▷ Liquid measuring cup

▷ Spider skimmer or colander

Start Cooking!

1. Add truffle paste, anchovy, garlic, and ¼ cup water to food processor. Lock lid into place. Hold down pulse button for 1 second, then release. Repeat pulsing until combined, about three 1-second pulses.

2. Turn on processor; pour oil through feed tube; and process unil rough sauce forms (like pesto!), about 30 seconds. Stop processor, remove lid, and carefully remove processor blade (ask an adult for help).

3. Use rubber spatula to transfer sauce to 11-inch sauté pan, making sure to scrape out all the sauce.

4. Add remaining 4 quarts water to large pot. Bring to a boil over high heat. Carefully add salt and then pasta to pot. Cook, stirring often with wooden spoon, until pasta is al dente (tender but still a bit chewy), 10 to 12 minutes. Turn off heat.

5. Use ladle to carefully transfer ⅓ cup pasta cooking water to liquid measuring cup. Use spider skimmer to transfer pasta to sauté pan with sauce (if you don't have a spider skimmer, ask an adult to drain the pasta in a colander in the sink).

6. Add reserved cooking water and cold butter to sauté pan. Cook over medium heat, stirring often, until sauce is emulsified (see "All About Emulsions," page 69) and pasta is well coated with sauce, about 2 minutes. Turn off heat. Season with salt and pepper to taste (see page 15). Serve with Parmesan.

From Chef Ken: The Other Truffles

This dish comes from the town of Norcia, Italy. Food-wise, Norcia is known for two things: fresh and cured pork products, such as sausages and salami, and truffles. No, not the chocolate candies—these truffles are a very rare species of mushroom that grows in damp forests. They're prized for their aroma (smell). In the past, truffle hunters used pigs to help sniff out these famous fungi, but today dogs are the more common helpers. In Norcia, when truffles are in season (in the fall), you'll see pasta dishes served with thin slices of truffle on top. Since fresh truffles are very expensive, and their flavor doesn't last for more than a few days, I like to use jarred black truffle paste. It lasts longer and still packs a lot of truffle flavor.

Spaghetti with Squid Ink Sauce

The cool color of this pasta sauce comes from an awesome ingredient: squid ink! It's the darkest black you can imagine, and its flavor is savory and slightly salty. The color covers the pasta, making the dish look kind of spooky (in a good way!). After you eat it, take a peek in the mirror, it might look like you have no teeth! But don't worry, the color comes off when you drink some water or brush your teeth. You can find squid ink at your local fishmonger, at specialty food stores, or online. Be careful when working with it because it can stain surfaces or clothes! You can use 1/3 cup clam juice or chicken broth instead of the wine in this recipe, if desired. For information on our favorite gluten-free pasta, see page 12.

Prepare Ingredients

- ¼ cup extra-virgin olive oil
- 1 small onion, peeled and chopped fine (see page 17)
- 3 garlic cloves, peeled and minced (see page 17)
- ⅛ teaspoon pepper
  Pinch crushed red pepper flakes
- ¼ teaspoon plus 2 tablespoons kosher salt, measured separately
- 3 tablespoons tomato paste
- ⅓ cup (2⅔ ounces) white wine (see note, below left)
- 2 tablespoons squid ink
- 1 tablespoon lemon juice, squeezed from ½ lemon
- ½ teaspoon fish sauce
- 4 quarts water
- 12 ounces gluten-free spaghetti

Gather Cooking Equipment

- ▷ 11-inch sauté pan or 12-inch skillet
- ▷ Wooden spoon
- ▷ Colander
- ▷ Large pot
- ▷ Ladle
- ▷ Liquid measuring cup
- ▷ Tongs

Start Cooking!

1. In 11-inch sauté pan combine oil and onion. Cook over medium heat, stirring occasionally with wooden spoon, until softened, about 5 minutes.

2. Add garlic, pepper, pepper flakes, and ¼ teaspoon salt and cook for 30 seconds. Stir in tomato paste and cook for 1 minute.

3. Stir in wine and cook for 1 minute. Add squid ink, lemon juice, and fish sauce and stir to combine. Turn off heat.

4. Place colander in sink. Add water to large pot. Bring to a boil over high heat. Carefully add remaining 2 tablespoons salt and then pasta to pot. Cook, stirring often with clean wooden spoon, until pasta is al dente (tender but still a bit chewy), 10 to 12 minutes. Turn off heat.

5. Use ladle to carefully transfer ¼ cup pasta cooking water to liquid measuring cup. Ask an adult to drain pasta in colander in sink. Transfer pasta to sauté pan with sauce and add reserved cooking water.

6. Cook over medium heat, tossing pasta with tongs, until pasta is well coated with sauce, about 2 minutes. Turn off heat. Season with salt and pepper to taste (see page 15). Serve.

ARE YOU SQUID-ING ME?!

Salty, briny, umami-tasting squid ink is the black-colored liquid that squid and other cephalopods, such as cuttlefish, release to avoid and confuse predators. (Much of the squid ink you can buy actually comes from cuttlefish, not squid!) In addition to pasta sauce, you'll also see squid ink used to make black-colored pasta dough and arroz negro ("black rice" paella).

Strawberry Shortcake Ice Cream Bars

When I was first diagnosed with celiac disease, I was probably the most sad about not being able to eat strawberry shortcake ice cream bars anymore. You know, the ones you get from the ice cream truck or a convenience store? The strawberry crumble on the outside is the best part, nothing else tastes like it—and it contains gluten. Eventually, my dad was able to crack the code and made this gluten-free version that tastes almost identical to the original. He even put them on the menu at his restaurant, Little Donkey! We recommend using a dense, premium ice cream such as Ben & Jerry's or Häagen-Dazs in this recipe, which helps the bars keep their shape. For information on substituting gluten-free flours, see page 12.

MAKES 6 bars
TOTAL TIME 1¾ hours, plus 6 hours chilling time

Prepare Ingredients

ICE CREAM AND STRAWBERRY CRUMBLES

2 pints vanilla ice cream

⅓ cup (1⅔ ounces) Cup4Cup Gluten-Free Multipurpose Flour

2 tablespoons cornstarch

2 tablespoons sugar

½ cup (1½ ounces) plus 2 tablespoons nonfat dry milk powder, measured separately

½ teaspoon kosher salt

4 tablespoons unsalted butter, melted (see page 16)

½ cup (¼ ounce) freeze-dried strawberries

3 tablespoons white chocolate chips

CHOCOLATE COATING

6 tablespoons (2¾ ounces) refined coconut oil

1 cup (6 ounces) white chocolate chips

Pinch kosher salt

Gather Cooking Equipment

▷ Spoon

▷ 6 ice pop molds, about 3 ounces each

▷ Skewer

▷ 6 ice pop sticks

▷ Rimmed baking sheet

▷ Parchment paper

▷ 2 bowls (1 large, 1 small microwave-safe)

▷ Whisk

▷ Oven mitts

▷ Cooling rack

▷ Large zipper-lock plastic bag

▷ Rolling pin

▷ Tall microwave-safe drinking glass

▷ Large plate

Start Cooking!

1. FOR THE ICE CREAM AND STRAWBERRY CRUMBLES: Remove ice cream from freezer and place in refrigerator. Let sit until softened, about 1½ hours.

2. Use spoon to fill each ice pop mold with softened ice cream, pushing down gently to fill molds completely. Use skewer to stir ice cream in molds to remove any air pockets. Add more ice cream as needed to fill molds all the way to edges.

3. Insert 1 ice pop stick in center of each mold and seal with cover. Freeze until firm, at least 4 hours or up to 24 hours.

4. Adjust oven rack to middle position and heat oven to 250 degrees. Line rimmed baking sheet with parchment paper.

5. In large bowl, whisk together flour, cornstarch, sugar, ½ cup milk powder, and ½ teaspoon salt. Add melted butter and whisk to combine. Use whisk to break any large pieces into fine crumbles.

Keep Going!

6. Transfer crumbles to parchment-lined baking sheet. Place baking sheet in oven. Bake until dry and sandy, about 20 minutes.

7. Use oven mitts to remove baking sheet from oven and place on cooling rack (ask an adult for help). Let crumbles cool completely, about 15 minutes. Transfer crumbles to clean large bowl.

8. Place strawberries in large zipper-lock plastic bag and seal bag, pressing out as much air as possible. Use rolling pin to gently crush freeze-dried strawberries into small pieces.

9. Sprinkle crushed strawberries and remaining 2 tablespoons milk powder evenly over crumbles and stir with clean, dry spoon until crumbles are well coated.

10. Place 3 tablespoons white chocolate chips in small microwave-safe bowl. Heat in microwave at 50 percent power for 30 seconds. Stop microwave and stir with spoon to combine. Continue to heat in microwave at 50 percent power until melted, 30 seconds to 1 minute. Remove bowl from microwave and stir until completely melted and smooth.

11. Drizzle melted white chocolate over crumbles. Use your fingers to rub chocolate into mixture until all crumbles are coated. (Crumbles can be stored in an airtight container at room temperature for up to 3 weeks.)

12. FOR THE CHOCOLATE COATING: When ready to assemble bars, transfer crumbles back to rimmed baking sheet and spread into even layer.

13. In tall microwave-safe drinking glass, combine coconut oil, 1 cup white chocolate chips, and pinch salt. Heat in microwave at 50 percent power for 1 minute. Stop microwave and stir with clean spoon to combine. Continue to heat in microwave at 50 percent power until melted, about 1 minute. Remove glass from microwave and stir until completely melted and smooth; set aside.

14. Line large plate with parchment paper and place in freezer. Working with 1 ice pop mold at a time, hold molds under warm running water for 30 seconds to thaw slightly, then slide ice cream bars from molds and place on parchment-lined plate in freezer. Let bars chill in freezer until firm, 5 to 10 minutes.

15. Working quickly, dip 1 frozen bar in white chocolate coating, then roll in strawberry crumbles following photos, below right. Return coated bar to parchment-lined plate in freezer. Repeat dipping and coating with remaining ice cream bars.

16. Chill bars until firm, 5 to 10 minutes. Serve. (Bars can be frozen for up to 24 hours.)

From Chef Ken: Re-creating a Classic

When Verveine was first diagnosed with celiac disease, she was so bummed that she couldn't eat strawberry shortcake bars anymore. I set out on a mission to create a gluten-free version of Verveine's favorite frozen treat. I used a mix of gluten-free flour and cornstarch to make the strawberry crumbles extra-crunchy. And for the perfect chocolate coating, I combined white chocolate with coconut oil. Coconut oil is liquid when it's warm and solid when it's room temperature or colder. And the colder it gets, the more brittle it becomes. So when the chocolate–coconut oil mixture hits the freezer, it forms a thin shell around the ice cream, just like the bars you buy.

How to Coat Ice Cream Bars

1. Working quickly, dip 1 frozen bar into white chocolate coating in drinking glass until covered. Lift bar out of chocolate and quickly shake from side to side to allow extra chocolate to drip off.

2. Immediately roll bar in strawberry crumbles on rimmed baking sheet, using your hand to scoop and press crumbles onto bar, until evenly coated. Place on parchment-lined plate in freezer. Repeat steps 1 and 2 with remaining bars.

Chapter 6

Desserts

Triple Chocolate Brownies

These are a variation of my Aunt Barrie's brownies (she's my dad's sister). When I was getting into cooking, I asked her for the recipe, and eventually, my dad and I came up with this extra-chocolaty version of her brownies. They're called "triple-chocolate" because they use three kinds of chocolate: semisweet chocolate chips, milk chocolate chips, and cocoa powder. For information on substituting gluten-free flours, see page 12.

MAKES 16 brownies
TOTAL TIME 1¼ hours, plus 1½ hours cooling time

Prepare Ingredients

Vegetable oil spray

12 tablespoons unsalted butter, cut into 12 pieces

6 tablespoons (2¼ ounces) semisweet chocolate chips

¼ cup (1½ ounces) milk chocolate chips

3 large eggs

1 cup (7 ounces) granulated sugar

¼ cup packed (1¾ ounces) brown sugar

1 teaspoon vanilla extract

¼ teaspoon kosher salt

¾ cup (2¼ ounces) unsweetened cocoa powder

½ cup (2½ ounces) Cup4Cup Gluten-Free Multipurpose Flour

Gather Cooking Equipment

▷ 8-inch square metal baking pan

▷ Parchment paper

▷ Medium microwave-safe bowl

▷ Rubber spatula

▷ Electric mixer (stand mixer with paddle attachment or handheld mixer and large bowl)

▷ Toothpick

▷ Oven mitts

▷ Cooling rack

▷ Cutting board

▷ Chef's knife

Start Cooking!

1. Adjust oven rack to middle position and heat oven to 350 degrees. Spray 8-inch square metal baking pan well with vegetable oil spray. Make parchment sling for baking pan (see photos, page 189). Spray parchment well with vegetable oil spray.

2. In medium microwave-safe bowl, combine butter, semisweet chocolate chips, and milk chocolate chips. Heat in microwave at 50 percent power for 1 minute. Stop microwave and stir mixture with rubber spatula to combine. Continue to heat in microwave at 50 percent power until melted, 1 to 2 minutes. Remove bowl from microwave and stir until completely melted and smooth. Set aside.

3. In bowl of stand mixer (or large bowl if using handheld mixer), combine eggs, granulated sugar, brown sugar, vanilla, and salt. Lock bowl into place and attach paddle to stand mixer, if using. Start mixer on medium speed and beat until very creamy and thickened, about 4 minutes. Stop mixer.

4. Add chocolate mixture. Start mixer on medium speed and beat until smooth, about 30 seconds. Stop mixer.

5. Add cocoa and flour. Start mixer on low speed and mix until well combined and smooth, about 30 seconds. Stop mixer. Remove bowl from stand mixer, if using.

6. Use rubber spatula to scrape down sides of bowl and stir in any remaining dry flour. Scrape batter into greased parchment-lined baking pan and spread into even layer.

7. Place baking pan in oven. Bake until toothpick inserted into center comes out with moist crumbs attached, 32 to 36 minutes.

8. Use oven mitts to remove baking pan from oven and place on cooling rack (ask an adult for help). Let brownies cool completely in pan on rack, about 1½ hours.

9. Use parchment sling to lift brownies out of pan and place on cutting board. Cut into squares and serve. (To cut squares with the sharpest sides, refrigerate the cooled brownies for 1 hour before cutting.)

Céline's Lemon Squares

This recipe is named after my mom, Céline, because she's made these lemon bars for as long as I can remember. They have a crust that isn't too sweet and a filling that has exactly the right amount of lemon. Each bar also has the perfect balance of textures: a smooth, creamy filling that's firmer on the surface and a crisp, buttery crust. For information on substituting gluten-free flours, see page 12.

Prepare Ingredients

CRUST

    Vegetable oil spray

8   tablespoons unsalted butter, cut into ½-inch pieces and chilled

1   cup (5 ounces) Cup4Cup Gluten-Free Multipurpose Flour

¼   cup (1 ounce) confectioners' (powdered) sugar

LEMON FILLING

1   cup (7 ounces) granulated sugar

2   large eggs

2   teaspoons grated lemon zest plus 3 tablespoons lemon juice, zested and squeezed from 1 lemon

½   teaspoon baking powder

¼   cup (1¼ ounces) Cup4Cup Gluten-Free Multipurpose Flour

1–2   teaspoons confectioners' (powdered) sugar, for dusting (optional)

Gather Cooking Equipment

▷   8-inch square metal baking pan

▷   Parchment paper

▷   Food processor

▷   Rubber spatula

▷   Oven mitts

▷   Cooling rack

▷   2 bowls (1 medium, 1 small)

▷   Whisk

▷   Butter knife

▷   Cutting board

▷   Chef's knife

▷   Fine-mesh strainer

Start Cooking!

1. FOR THE CRUST: Adjust oven rack to middle position and heat oven to 350 degrees. Spray 8-inch square metal baking pan well with vegetable oil spray. Make parchment sling for baking pan (see photos, page 189). Spray parchment well with vegetable oil spray.

2. Add butter, 1 cup flour, and ¼ cup confectioners' sugar to food processor. Lock lid into place. Hold down pulse button for 1 second, then release. Repeat until butter is broken down into small pieces and ingredients are well combined, fifteen to twenty 1-second pulses. Remove lid and carefully remove processor blade (ask an adult for help).

3. Use rubber spatula to transfer mixture to greased parchment-lined baking pan. Spread into even layer covering bottom of baking pan and use your hands to press flat.

4. Place baking pan in oven. Bake until crust is light golden, about 20 minutes.

5. Use oven mitts to remove baking pan from oven and place on cooling rack (ask an adult for help). Reduce oven temperature to 325 degrees. Let crust cool for at least 15 minutes.

Keep Going!

6. FOR THE LEMON FILLING: While crust is cooling, in medium bowl, whisk granulated sugar and eggs until well combined. Add lemon zest and juice, baking powder, and ¼ cup flour, and whisk until smooth.

7. Pour filling on top of cooled crust. Carefully spread into even layer with clean rubber spatula (be careful—baking pan will be warm).

8. Place baking pan in oven. Bake until filling is set, about 30 minutes.

9. Use oven mitts to remove baking pan from oven and place on cooling rack (ask an adult for help). Let lemon squares cool completely in pan, about 1½ hours.

10. Run butter knife around edges of pan to loosen. Use parchment sling to lift lemon squares out of pan and place on cutting board. Use chef's knife to cut into squares. Dust with 1 to 2 teaspoons confectioners' sugar (if using—see photos, below right). Serve. (If you like your lemon squares cold, you can refrigerate them for at least 1 hour before cutting and serving).

From Chef Ken: No-Cook Curd

In a lot of recipes for lemon squares, you need to cook the filling—also known as lemon curd—until it's thick but still pourable. And then you still need to bake it until it's solid and sliceable. But not in this recipe. By using less water (the water comes from the lemon juice and egg yolks) and a little more flour and sugar than most other lemon curd recipes, our filling is nice and thick after just whisking the ingredients together. And after baking, it's perfectly set and sliceable.

How to Make a Parchment Sling

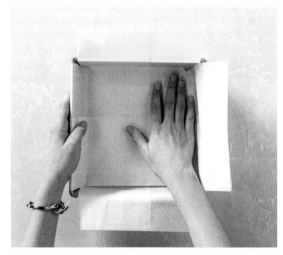

1. Fold 2 long sheets of parchment paper so that both sheets measure 8 inches across (sheets should match width of baking pan).

2. Lay sheets of parchment in pan so that sheets are perpendicular to each other. Let extra parchment hang over edges of pan. Push parchment into corners and up sides of pan, smoothing parchment so that it rests against pan.

How to Dust with Confectioners' Sugar or Cocoa Powder

1. Set fine-mesh strainer over small bowl. Add 1 to 2 teaspoons confectioners' sugar to strainer.

2. Use strainer to dust confectioners' sugar evenly over lemon squares, gently tapping side of strainer to release sugar.

Rugelach

This is another one of my mom's recipes. (Can you tell she's the biggest baker in our family?) These cookies look like little snail shells with their spirals of filling. Not only are they pretty to look at, but their flavor is the perfect combination of butter, sugar, and cinnamon, and they have a texture that melts in your mouth. I think it's interesting that the dough doesn't have any sugar in it—all the sweetness comes from the cinnamon-sugar-walnut filling. For information on substituting gluten-free flours, see page 12.

MAKES 16 rugelach
TOTAL TIME 45 minutes, plus 2½ hours chilling and cooling time

Prepare Ingredients

DOUGH

4   ounces cream cheese, cut into 8 pieces and chilled

8   tablespoons unsalted butter, cut into 8 pieces and chilled

1   cup (5 ounces) Cup4Cup Gluten-Free Multipurpose Flour, plus extra for counter

⅛   teaspoon kosher salt

FILLING

½   cup (3½ ounces) sugar

⅓   cup walnuts

1   tablespoon ground cinnamon

Gather Cooking Equipment

▷   Food processor

▷   Bench scraper or butter knife

▷   Ruler

▷   Plastic wrap

▷   Rimmed baking sheet

▷   Parchment paper

▷   Medium bowl

▷   Rolling pin

▷   Ruler

▷   Spoon

▷   Chef's knife

▷   Oven mitts

▷   Cooling rack

▷   Spatula

Start Cooking!

1. FOR THE DOUGH: Add all dough ingredients to food processor. Lock lid into place. Turn on processor and process until dough forms, about 30 seconds. Stop processor. Remove lid and carefully remove processor blade (ask an adult for help).

2. Sprinkle clean counter with extra flour and transfer dough to counter. Use your hands to knead dough until it comes together into ball. Use bench scraper to cut dough in half. Pat each piece into 4-inch square and wrap each square in plastic wrap. Place dough in refrigerator to chill for at least 2 hours or up to 24 hours.

3. FOR THE FILLING: Adjust oven rack to middle position and heat oven to 400 degrees. Line rimmed baking sheet with parchment paper.

4. Add sugar, walnuts, and cinnamon to clean food processor. Lock lid into place. Turn on processor and process until nuts are finely ground, about 15 seconds. Stop processor. Remove lid and carefully remove processor blade (ask an adult for help). Transfer filling to medium bowl.

5. Unwrap chilled dough squares and discard plastic wrap. Roll, fill, shape, and cut rugelach following photos, page 192.

6. Place baking sheet in oven. Bake until rugelach are deep golden brown and sugar is caramelized (turns golden brown), 15 to 18 minutes.

7. Use oven mitts to remove baking sheet from oven and place on cooling rack (ask an adult for help). Let rugelach cool on baking sheet for 10 minutes. Use spatula to transfer rugelach directly to cooling rack. Let rugelach cool completely, about 20 minutes. Serve.

Keep Going!

From Chef Ken: Cream Cheese in Cookie Dough?

These rolled, filled cookies are popular in Jewish bakeries around the world. To me, they taste just like amped-up Cinnamon Toast Crunch cereal. The cream cheese makes the dough soft and easy to roll out, plus it gives it a hint of tang to balance all that sweetness in the filling.

How to Shape Rugelach

1. Sprinkle clean counter with a little bit of filling, and place 1 dough square on top. Sprinkle dough with a little bit of filling. Use rolling pin to roll dough into 8-inch square, about ¼ inch thick.

2. Spoon half of filling onto dough, spreading it all the way to the edges (it's OK if filling spills over edges a little bit). Press filling into dough so that it sticks.

3. Starting with side closest to you, gently roll dough into log, pinching any cracks closed. (If using a flour other than Cup4Cup Gluten-Free Multipurpose Flour, your dough may crack more.) Gather up extra filling from counter, sprinkle evenly over top of dough log, and press so that it sticks.

4. Use chef's knife to cut dough log crosswise (the short way) into 8 equal pieces. Place rugelach upright on parchment-lined baking sheet, leaving space between cookies. Repeat rolling, filling, shaping, and cutting with second piece of dough and remaining filling.

Baci di Dama

I mean it with all my heart: These little Nutella sandwich cookies are my favorite dessert. I first had baci di dama at a restaurant on the border of France and Italy. Our server gave each of us a cookie with the check. As soon as we tasted them we had to ask the server for the recipe—and luckily, she gave it to us. We started trying them at different bakeries during our trip, but none were as good as those first cookies. Since then, we've made baci di dama for every occasion we can. Do not use almond flour labeled "superfine" in this recipe. For information on substituting gluten-free flours, see page 12.

MAKES 24 sandwich cookies
TOTAL TIME 1½ hours, plus cooling time

Prepare Ingredients

1   cup (3½ ounces) blanched almond flour

¾   cup (3¾ ounces) Cup4Cup Gluten-Free Multipurpose Flour

½   cup (3½ ounces) sugar

8   tablespoons unsalted butter, cut into 8 pieces

¾   teaspoon kosher salt

½   teaspoon vanilla extract

⅓   cup (3½ ounces) Nutella

Gather Cooking Equipment

▷ Rimmed baking sheet

▷ Parchment paper

▷ Food processor

▷ Rubber spatula

▷ Medium bowl

▷ 1-teaspoon measuring spoon

▷ Oven mitts

▷ Cooling rack

▷ Spoon

▷ Quart-size zipper-lock plastic bag

▷ Scissors

▷ Ruler

Start Cooking!

1. Adjust oven rack to middle position and heat oven to 275 degrees. Line rimmed baking sheet with parchment paper.

2. Add almond flour, Cup4Cup gluten-free flour, sugar, butter, salt, and vanilla to food processor. Lock lid into place. Turn on processor and process until mixture comes together and smooth dough forms, about 1 minute. Stop processor. Remove lid and carefully remove processor blade (ask an adult for help).

3. Use rubber spatula to transfer dough to medium bowl. Use your hands to roll dough into 48 balls (about 1 heaping teaspoon each). Place dough balls on parchment-lined baking sheet, leaving space between balls.

4. Place baking sheet in oven. Bake cookies until light golden brown and firm, 30 to 35 minutes.

5. Use oven mitts to remove baking sheet from oven and place on cooling rack (ask an adult for help). Let cookies cool completely on baking sheet, about 20 minutes.

6. Use spoon to scoop Nutella into quart-size zipper-lock plastic bag. Squeeze and push Nutella into one corner of bag. Twist top of bag nice and tight. Use scissors to snip ⅛ inch off corner of filled bag.

7. Flip half of cooled cookies over on baking sheet. Fill and assemble baci di dama following photos, below. Serve.

How to Fill and Assemble Baci di Dama

1. Squeeze a dime-size amount of Nutella onto each of the 24 upside-down cookies.

2. Place second cookie on top of each filled cookie and press down gently to make sandwich.

Funfetti Cupcakes

For as long as I can remember, funfetti cake or cupcakes has been the go-to dessert for my birthday and my brother's birthday. I'll tell you a secret: I have a weakness for sprinkles . . . and who wouldn't love cupcakes that are filled with them? I recommend using vanilla frosting and then decorating with even more sprinkles, but you can use your favorite frosting and decorations. Don't be afraid to go all out, it's a celebration, after all! For information on substituting gluten-free flours, see page 12.

MAKES 12 cupcakes
TOTAL TIME 1 hour, plus cooling time

Prepare Ingredients

Vegetable oil spray

10 tablespoons unsalted butter, softened (see page 16)

1 cup (7 ounces) sugar

3 large eggs

½ teaspoon vanilla extract

1½ cups (7½ ounces) Cup4Cup Gluten-Free Multipurpose flour

1½ teaspoons baking powder

¼ teaspoon xanthan gum

¼ teaspoon kosher salt

⅓ cup plus 1 tablespoon rainbow sprinkles, measured separately

1½ cups store-bought frosting (your favorite flavor!)

Gather Cooking Equipment

▷ 12-cup muffin tin

▷ 12 paper cupcake liners

▷ Food processor

▷ Rubber spatula

▷ Medium bowl

▷ ¼-cup dry measuring cup

▷ Toothpick

▷ Oven mitts

▷ Cooling rack

▷ 1-tablespoon measuring spoon

▷ Small icing (offset) spatula or spoon

Start Cooking!

1. Adjust oven rack to middle position and heat oven to 325 degrees. Line 12-cup muffin tin with paper cupcake liners and spray with vegetable oil spray.

2. Add softened butter and sugar to food processor. Lock lid into place. Turn on processor and process until light and fluffy, about 30 seconds.

3. Stop processor and remove lid. Add 1 egg and vanilla and lock lid back into place. Turn on processor and process until well combined, about 10 seconds. Stop processor and remove lid. Use rubber spatula to scrape down sides of food processor bowl. Repeat with remaining 2 eggs, adding them one at a time and scraping down bowl after each addition.

4. Add flour, baking powder, xanthan gum, and salt and lock lid back into place. Turn on processor and process until well combined, about 30 seconds.

5. Stop processor, remove lid, and carefully remove processor blade (ask an adult for help). Scrape batter into medium bowl. Add ⅓ cup sprinkles and gently stir to combine.

6. Use ¼-cup dry measuring cup to divide batter evenly among muffin cups.

7. Place muffin tin in oven. Bake until toothpick inserted in center of 1 cupcake comes out clean, about 24 minutes.

8. Use oven mitts to remove muffin tin from oven and place on cooling rack (ask an adult for help). Let cupcakes cool in muffin tin for 15 minutes.

9. Remove cupcakes from muffin tin and transfer directly to cooling rack. Let cupcakes cool completely, about 30 minutes.

10. Frost cupcakes following photos, page 198. Sprinkle with remaining 1 tablespoon sprinkles. Serve.

Keep Going!

How to Frost Cupcakes

1. Mound 2 tablespoons frosting in center of cupcake.

2. Use icing spatula to spread frosting to edge of cupcake, leaving slight mound of frosting in center. Keep frosting off paper liner.

Molten Chocolate Cakes with Peanut Butter Sauce

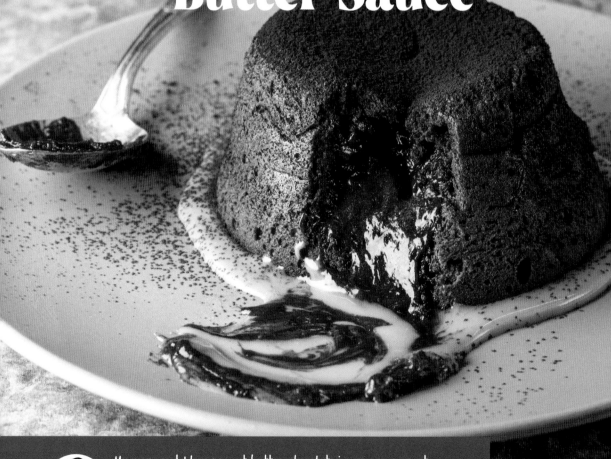

My mom and I love peanut butter–chocolate ice cream, peanut butter–chocolate cookies, and even just a piece of chocolate with peanut butter on it. This recipe is for everyone like my mom and me, who can never say no to peanut butter and chocolate! It combines a molten chocolate cake (a cake that, when you cut into it, has a warm chocolate filling that runs out) with a delicious peanut butter sauce. (If you have leftover peanut butter sauce, I recommend putting it on vanilla ice cream.) For information on substituting gluten-free flours, see page 12.

SERVES 4
TOTAL TIME 50 minutes

Prepare Ingredients

CAKES
Vegetable oil spray

8 tablespoons unsalted butter, cut into 8 pieces

1 cup (6 ounces) bittersweet chocolate chips

2 large eggs plus 2 large egg yolks (see page 16)

¼ cup (1¾ ounces) sugar

Pinch kosher salt

2 tablespoons Cup4Cup Gluten-Free Multipurpose Flour

Cocoa powder, for dusting

PEANUT BUTTER SAUCE
1 (14-ounce) can sweetened condensed milk

⅓ cup creamy peanut butter

⅛ teaspoon kosher salt

Gather Cooking Equipment

▷ 4 (4-ounce) ramekins

▷ 2 bowls (1 medium microwave-safe, 1 small)

▷ Rubber spatula

▷ Electric mixer (stand mixer with whisk attachment or handheld mixer and large bowl)

▷ Spoon

▷ Rimmed baking sheet

▷ Oven mitts

▷ Cooling rack

▷ Small saucepan

▷ Serving plates

▷ Fine-mesh strainer

Start Cooking!

1. FOR THE CAKES: Adjust oven rack to middle position and heat oven to 450 degrees. Spray four 4-ounce ramekins with vegetable oil spray.

2. In medium microwave-safe bowl, combine butter and chocolate chips. Heat in microwave at 50 percent power for 1 minute. Stop microwave and stir mixture with rubber spatula to combine. Continue to heat in microwave at 50 percent power until melted, 1 to 2 minutes. Remove bowl from microwave and stir until completely melted and smooth.

3. In bowl of stand mixer (or large bowl if using handheld mixer), combine eggs and egg yolks, sugar, and pinch salt. Lock bowl into place and attach whisk attachment to mixer, if using. Start mixer on high speed and beat until thickened and light yellow in color, about 2 minutes. Stop mixer.

4. Add flour and melted chocolate mixture. Start mixer on medium speed and beat until combined, 30 seconds to 1 minute. Stop mixer and remove bowl from stand mixer, if using.

5. Use spoon to divide batter evenly among greased ramekins. Place ramekins on rimmed baking sheet.

6. Place baking sheet in oven. Bake until sides of cakes are firm but centers are still soft, 6 to 9 minutes.

7. Use oven mitts to remove baking sheet from oven and place on cooling rack (ask an adult for help). Let cakes cool for 5 minutes.

8. FOR THE PEANUT BUTTER SAUCE: While cakes are cooling, in small saucepan use clean rubber spatula to stir condensed milk, peanut butter, and ⅛ teaspoon salt until well combined. Cook over low heat, stirring and scraping bottom of pan, until warmed through, about 3 minutes. Turn off heat.

9. Use clean spoon to make small pool of sauce on each serving plate. Ask an adult to flip each cake out of ramekin onto sauce (be careful—ramekins will be hot). Dust each cake with cocoa powder following photos, page 189. Serve immediately. (Peanut butter sauce can be refrigerated in an airtight container for up to 1 week. Reheat before using.)

Lemon Pound Cake

If you love lemon, you're going to love this cake. Besides being a delicious, lemony cake, it also has a lemon-sugar glaze. It's fun to poke holes in the cake, pour on the glaze, and see it soak in, but my favorite part is how some of the glaze crystallizes on the surface of the cake. It creates this sparkly, sugary layer that adds another texture to this dessert. For information on substituting gluten-free flours, see page 12.

SERVES 12 to 14
TOTAL TIME 1¾ hours, plus 1 hour cooling time

Prepare Ingredients

CAKE

Vegetable oil spray

3   cups (15 ounces) Cup4Cup Gluten-Free Multipurpose Flour

2   teaspoons baking powder

½   teaspoon kosher salt

16 tablespoons unsalted butter, cut into 16 pieces and softened (see page 16)

2   cups (14 ounces) sugar

4   large eggs

1   cup (8 ounces) milk

4   teaspoons grated lemon zest, zested from 2 lemons

GLAZE

⅓   cup lemon juice, squeezed from 2 lemons

¾   cup (5¼ ounces) sugar

Gather Cooking Equipment

▷ 10-cup tube pan

▷ Medium bowl

▷ Whisk

▷ Electric mixer (stand mixer with paddle attachment or handheld mixer and large bowl)

▷ Rubber spatula

▷ Toothpick

▷ Oven mitts

▷ Cooling rack

▷ Liquid measuring cup

▷ Spoon

▷ Butter knife

Start Cooking!

1. FOR THE CAKE: Adjust oven rack to middle position and heat oven to 350 degrees. Spray 10-cup tube pan with vegetable oil spray.

2. In medium bowl, whisk together flour, baking powder, and salt.

3. In bowl of stand mixer (or large bowl if using handheld mixer), combine softened butter and 2 cups sugar. Lock bowl into place and attach paddle attachment to stand mixer, if using. Start mixer on low speed and beat until combined. Increase speed to medium-high and beat until mixture is light and fluffy, 2 to 3 minutes.

4. Stop mixer and use rubber spatula to scrape down sides of bowl. Start mixer on medium speed and add eggs, one at a time, and beat until combined, about 1 minute.

5. Stop mixer and use rubber spatula to scrape down sides of bowl. Carefully add half of flour mixture. Start mixer on low speed and mix until just combined, about 30 seconds. With mixer running, slowly add milk and lemon zest and mix until combined, about 30 seconds. Stop mixer.

6. Add remaining flour mixture. Start mixer on low speed and mix until just combined and no dry flour is visible, about 30 seconds. Stop mixer. Remove bowl from stand mixer, if using.

7. Use rubber spatula to scrape down sides of bowl and stir in any remaining dry flour. Scrape batter into greased tube pan and smooth top.

8. Place tube pan in oven. Bake until golden brown and toothpick inserted in center comes out clean, about 1 hour.

9. Use oven mitts to remove tube pan from oven and place on cooling rack (ask an adult for help). Let cake cool for 5 minutes.

10. FOR THE GLAZE: In liquid measuring cup, use spoon to stir lemon juice and ¾ cup sugar until well combined. Poke cake with butter knife and pour glaze over top following photos, page 204.

11. Let cake cool completely in pan, about 1 hour. Use butter knife to slice cake in pan. Serve.

Keep Going!

How to Soak Pound Cake with Glaze

1. Use butter knife to poke about 20 holes in cake (be careful—tube pan will be hot).

2. Pour glaze evenly over top of cake and poke a few more holes in cake to allow glaze to fully soak in.

3. Run butter knife around edge of cake to loosen from pan and allow glaze to run down sides.

How Pound Cake Got Its Name

 OK Dad, I've got another culinary conundrum for you: Why is a pound cake called a pound cake? Is it because the cake weighs a pound?

 You're close! The first versions of this recipe, from way back in the 1700s, called for 1 pound of butter, 1 pound of sugar, 1 pound of flour, and 1 pound of eggs. Hence, "pound cake."

 Uh, that sounds like it would make a VERY big cake, not that I would mind.

 Yeah, over the years the recipe was scaled down a bit and some more ingredients were added, like the baking powder that helps this cake rise.

 Well, I still think I could eat a pound of this cake—it's so lemony and delicious.

Quatre Quart with Chocolate Ganache

My great-grandma passed this buttery French cake recipe down to my grandma, who passed it down to my mom, who passed it down to me, who had to change it! At the time, I was really into the combination of molasses, ginger, and cocoa powder, so I added some of each to the original recipe. When I put the cake in the oven, I was nervous because it was brown instead of the usual bright yellow. But I didn't need to worry, because it was delicious! We prefer Dutch-processed cocoa powder in this recipe. You can use natural cocoa powder, but your cake will be drier in texture and lighter in color. You can decorate your cake with crushed candy canes or finely chopped white chocolate after adding the ganache in step 11. For information on substituting gluten-free flours, see page 12.

SERVES 12
TOTAL TIME 2 hours, plus 1¼ hours cooling time

Prepare Ingredients

CAKE

Vegetable oil spray

1 cup (7 ounces) sugar

16 tablespoons unsalted butter, cut into 16 pieces and softened (see page 16)

2 large eggs

1 cup (5 ounces) Cup4Cup Gluten-Free Multipurpose Flour

2 tablespoons Dutch-processed cocoa powder

2 tablespoons molasses

1 teaspoon vanilla extract

1 teaspoon baking powder

1 teaspoon ground ginger

GANACHE

½ cup (4 ounces) heavy cream

1½ teaspoons maple syrup

1½ teaspoons honey

⅛ teaspoon espelette pepper (optional) (see "Glorious Ganache," page 208)

1 cup (6 ounces) bittersweet chocolate chips

½ tablespoon unsalted butter, softened

1 tablespoon demerara sugar (optional)

Gather Cooking Equipment

▷ 8-inch springform pan or 8-inch round metal cake pan lined with parchment paper

▷ Food processor

▷ Rubber spatula

▷ Toothpick

▷ Oven mitts

▷ Cooling rack

▷ Small saucepan

▷ Medium heatproof bowl

▷ Icing (offset) spatula

▷ Serving platter

▷ Chef's knife

Start Cooking!

1. FOR THE CAKE: Adjust oven rack to middle position and heat oven to 350 degrees. Spray 8-inch springform pan with vegetable oil spray.

2. Add sugar and 16 tablespoons softened butter to food processor. Lock lid into place. Turn on processor and process until light and fluffy, about 30 seconds.

3. Stop processor and remove lid. Add eggs and lock lid back into place. Turn on processor and process until well combined, about 10 seconds.

4. Stop processor and remove lid. Use rubber spatula to scrape down sides of processor bowl. Add flour, cocoa, molasses, vanilla, baking powder, and ginger and lock lid back into place. Turn on processor and process until well combined, about 30 seconds.

5. Stop processor, remove lid, and carefully remove processor blade (ask an adult for help). Use rubber spatula to scrape batter into greased springform pan and smooth into even layer.

6. Place springform pan in oven. Bake until toothpick inserted in center comes out clean, 45 to 50 minutes.

Keep Going!

7. Use oven mitts to remove springform pan from oven and place on cooling rack (ask an adult for help). Let cake cool for 15 minutes.

8. Remove side of springform pan (ask an adult for help—pan will be hot). Let cake cool completely on cooling rack, about 1 hour.

9. **FOR THE GANACHE:** In small saucepan, combine cream, maple syrup, honey, and espelette pepper (if using). Cook over medium heat until steaming and just beginning to bubble, 2 to 4 minutes. Turn off heat.

10. Make ganache following photos, below.

11. Slide icing spatula underneath cake to loosen from pan bottom, then transfer cake to serving platter. Pour ganache over cake and use clean icing spatula to spread into even layer over top, letting some ganache drip over the sides. Sprinkle demerara sugar (if using) over top. Cut cake into slices and serve.

From Chef Ken: Glorious Ganache

Ganache sounds fancy, but it's just the word for a mixture of melted chocolate and cream. If you change how much cream or chocolate you use, you'll get a ganache that's liquid and pourable like this one or one that sets up firm and solid when it cools. And ganache can be used for much more than glazing cakes! It makes the best chocolate fudge sauce for ice cream. You can turn it into amazing hot chocolate if you whisk in more hot milk or cream. You can even use it to create your own candy bars or truffles. I also love that you can flavor it with all sorts of ingredients, like the maple syrup, honey, and smoky-sweet espelette pepper in this recipe.

How to Make Ganache

If your chocolate isn't completely melted before you add the butter in step 2, heat it in the microwave at 50 percent power until it's melted, about 30 seconds.

1. Place chocolate chips in medium heatproof bowl and make small well in center. Pour about half of hot cream mixture into center of chocolate (ask an adult for help). Use clean rubber spatula to stir in small circles until center of chocolate is melted and liquid is smooth.

2. Pour remaining cream mixture into center of bowl and stir from center outwards, scraping unmelted chocolate chips from sides of bowl and stirring until mixture is completely smooth and shiny. Add ½ tablespoon softened butter and stir until well combined.

Apple Crumble

This is a simple recipe that never fails to be delicious. I think it has the perfect ratio of soft apples to crunchy crumble. Be sure to always serve your apple crumble warm! You can eat it on its own, but I think it's best with some vanilla or cinnamon ice cream. We prefer sweet apples in this recipe, such as Golden Delicious, Jonagold, or Braeburn. For information on substituting gluten-free flours, see page 12.

SERVES 8
TOTAL TIME 1¼ hours, plus cooling time

Prepare Ingredients

6 apples, peeled, cored, and cut into 1-inch pieces (see photo, below right)

¼ cup (1¾ ounces) plus ¼ cup (1¾ ounces) granulated sugar, measured separately

8 tablespoons unsalted butter, cut into 8 pieces and softened (see page 16)

1 cup (3 ounces) gluten-free oats

¾ cup (3¾ ounces) Cup4Cup Gluten-Free Multipurpose Flour

¼ cup packed (1¾ ounces) brown sugar

¼ teaspoon kosher salt

Gather Cooking Equipment

▷ 2 bowls (1 large, 1 medium)

▷ Rubber spatula

▷ 10-inch cast-iron skillet or 8-inch square baking dish

▷ Oven mitts

▷ Cooling rack

Start Cooking!

1. Adjust oven rack to middle position and heat oven to 350 degrees.

2. In large bowl, use rubber spatula to stir apples and ¼ cup granulated sugar until well combined. Transfer to 10-inch cast-iron skillet.

3. In medium bowl, combine softened butter, oats, flour, brown sugar, salt, and remaining ¼ cup granulated sugar. Use your fingers to rub softened butter into oat mixture until fully incorporated. Break topping into walnut-size pieces and sprinkle evenly over apples.

4. Place skillet in oven. Bake until filling is bubbling and topping is golden brown, 45 to 55 minutes.

5. Ask an adult to use oven mitts to remove skillet from oven and place on cooling rack (ask an adult for help). Place oven mitt on skillet handle so you remember handle is HOT. Let cool for at least 10 minutes. Serve warm.

How to Core and Chop Apples

Place peeled apple on cutting board. Use chef's knife to slice around core to remove 4 large pieces. Discard core. Place pieces flat side down on cutting board and chop into 1-inch pieces. Repeat with remaining apples.

A FAMILY OF FRUIT DESSERTS

The world of baked fruit desserts is wide! Here are just a few.

CRUMBLE OR CRISP
Fruit baked under a crunchy topping that usually contains oats

BUCKLE
Cake batter poured over fruit (usually berries) and baked

PIE
Fruit baked between layers of flaky pie dough

COBBLER
Biscuit dough dolloped over fruit and baked

Boba Drinks

Boba are little chewy, slightly sweet balls of tapioca that are often served in a drink. They're incredibly popular in Taiwan. There are also boba tea (or "bubble tea") shops in Boston, where I live. Milk tea is the most traditional drink to serve with boba, but you can use strawberry or chocolate milk, iced tea, lemonade, or fruit-flavored soda—black raspberry is my favorite! When you get boba tea from a store or stand, it's served with an extra-wide straw so that you can suck up the boba and drink the liquid. Look for dried black tapioca (boba) pearls in East Asian grocery stores or online. You can also spoon cooked boba over ice cream or eat a bowl of boba with a splash of sweetened coconut milk.

SERVES 2
TOTAL TIME 30 minutes, plus cooling time

Prepare Ingredients

½ cup packed (3½ ounces) brown sugar

½ cup plus 3 quarts water, measured separately

1 cup black tapioca (boba) pearls (see note, below left)

2 cups strawberry or chocolate milk, iced tea, lemonade, or fruit soda

Salted caramel sauce (see page 27) or chocolate syrup (optional)

Gather Cooking Equipment

▷ Small saucepan

▷ 2 bowls (1 medium, 1 medium heatproof)

▷ Large saucepan

▷ Spider skimmer or slotted spoon

▷ 2 tall drinking glasses

▷ Liquid measuring cup

▷ 2 wide straws (optional)

Start Cooking!

1. In small saucepan, combine brown sugar and ½ cup water. Cook over medium heat until sugar dissolves completely, about 2 minutes. Turn off heat. Carefully pour brown sugar–water mixture into medium heatproof bowl (this sugar-water mixture is known as simple syrup). Let cool completely, about 30 minutes.

2. In large saucepan, bring remaining 3 quarts water to a boil. Carefully add boba and gently stir with spider skimmer. Reduce heat to medium and cook until soft and translucent, 3 to 8 minutes (check package instructions for timing). Turn off heat.

3. Let boba sit in water for another 3 to 8 minutes (check package directions for timing); they will shrink and turn black and glossy (see photo below). While boba sit, fill medium bowl with cold water.

4. Use spider skimmer to transfer boba to cold water and let sit for 30 seconds. Immediately use spider skimmer to transfer boba to bowl with brown sugar simple syrup. (Boba are best served right away but can sit in simple syrup on counter for up to 8 hours before serving.)

5. Use spider skimmer to divide boba evenly between 2 tall drinking glasses. Pour 1 cup of your favorite drink into each glass and drizzle with salted caramel sauce (if using). Serve with wide straws (if using).

How to Tell When Boba Are Ready

Let boba sit in water for 3 to 8 minutes (check package directions for timing); they will shrink and turn black and glossy.

Lemon Italian Ice

Picture this: It's a hot summer day. You've been hanging out at the pool or ocean. You could really use something to cool you down right now. How about this refreshing lemon Italian ice? It's really easy to make and uses three ingredients that you probably have right now: water, lemons, and sugar. What are you waiting for? Go make it! (Unless it's winter. Then you might want to wait a few seasons.) For a fun way to serve this dessert, scoop out the insides of lemon halves and fill them with your Italian ice.

4 ⊞ **SERVES** 4 to 6 (Makes about 1 quart)
TOTAL TIME 20 minutes, plus 4 hours cooling and chilling time

Prepare Ingredients

4   cups (32 ounces) water

1   cup (7 ounces) sugar

2   teaspoons grated lemon zest plus ¾ cup lemon juice, zested and squeezed from 3 to 4 lemons

Gather Cooking Equipment

▷ Small saucepan

▷ Metal spoon

▷ 13-by-9-inch metal baking pan

Start Cooking!

1. In small saucepan, combine water and sugar. Cook over medium heat, stirring occasionally with metal spoon, until sugar dissolves, about 10 minutes.

2. Turn off heat and slide saucepan to cool burner. Add lemon zest and juice and stir to combine. Pour mixture into 13-by-9-inch metal baking pan. Let cool for 1 hour.

3. Carefully place baking pan in freezer and let chill for 30 minutes. Use metal spoon to stir lemon mixture and scrape edges of baking pan well. Smooth mixture back into even layer.

4. Continue to freeze until smooth and creamy, about 2½ hours, stirring every 30 minutes, making sure to scrape edges of pan well and spread mixture back into even layer each time. Serve. (Italian ice can be frozen for up to 1 week. If it becomes too hard, place in refrigerator for 30 to 45 minutes to soften slightly before serving.)

From Chef Ken: Sugary Science

Italian ice was invented by Italian immigrants living in the northeastern United States. It's very similar to Sicilian granita, another Italian frozen fruit dessert. And it's so easy to make. Just three ingredients create this amazing soft texture. The key to that texture is sugar. Without it, you'd have a lemon-flavored ice cube. Sugar makes Italian ice sweet and also makes it scoopable. The sugar dissolves into the water (lemon juice is mostly water). As the water-sugar mixture freezes, the dissolved sugar gets in the way of ice crystals forming. It also makes any ice crystals that do form very tiny. And lots of tiny ice crystals give you a smoother texture. The sugar also lowers the freezing point of the water to below 32 degrees Fahrenheit. That makes it harder for ice crystals to form at all, leaving you with a more spoonable, softer dessert.

Chocolate Chip Cookie Dough Ice Cream

I've always been a fan of ice cream with stuff mixed into it: peanut butter cups, mint chocolate chips, freeze-dried strawberries . . . but my personal favorite is cookie dough. With this recipe, you get to make both the ice cream AND the cookie dough yourself, which is fun and exciting. (Plus, you don't need a special ice cream maker, just a food processor.) If you'd prefer plain vanilla ice cream, you can skip adding the cookie dough.

Prepare Ingredients

- 5 large egg yolks (see page 16)
- ½ cup (3½ ounces) sugar
- ⅓ cup maple syrup
- 2 teaspoons vanilla extract
- ¼ teaspoon kosher salt
- 3 cups (24 ounces) heavy cream
- 3 ounces cream cheese, cut into ½-inch pieces and softened
- ⅓ cup (2⅔ ounces) milk
- 1 recipe Chocolate Chip Cookie Dough (page 219)

Gather Cooking Equipment

- ▷ 2 heatproof bowls (1 large, 1 medium)
- ▷ Whisk
- ▷ Medium saucepan
- ▷ Rubber spatula
- ▷ Instant-read thermometer
- ▷ Spoon
- ▷ Fine-mesh strainer
- ▷ 4-cup liquid measuring cup
- ▷ 3 ice cube trays
- ▷ Butter knife
- ▷ Food processor

Start Cooking!

1. In medium heatproof bowl, whisk egg yolks, sugar, maple syrup, vanilla, and salt until smooth.

2. In medium saucepan, bring cream to simmer over medium-low heat (small bubbles should break often across surface of cream), stirring occasionally with rubber spatula, 8 to 12 minutes. Turn off heat.

3. Ask an adult to slowly pour half of hot cream into egg yolk mixture, whisking constantly.

4. Pour egg yolk mixture back into saucepan with remaining cream. Whisk until well combined. Cook over low heat, stirring constantly and scraping bottom of pan with rubber spatula, until mixture thickens, registers 180 degrees on instant-read thermometer, and coats the back of a spoon, 8 to 10 minutes (see photo, page 218). (Do not let mixture come to boil.) Turn off heat and slide saucepan to cool burner.

5. Set fine-mesh strainer over large heatproof bowl. Ask an adult to pour cream mixture through strainer into bowl. Discard any solids in strainer. Add softened cream cheese to bowl and whisk until smooth.

6. Let cool until just warm, about 45 minutes. Transfer mixture to 4-cup liquid measuring cup. Pour mixture into 3 ice cube trays. Place in freezer and freeze until solid, at least 8 hours or overnight. (Now is a good time to make your cookie dough!)

7. Remove ice cube trays from freezer and let sit on counter until softened slightly, about 5 minutes (no longer or it will start to melt!).

8. Use butter knife to loosen cubes from ice cube trays. Transfer half of cubes to food processor. Add half of milk. Lock lid into place. Turn on processor and process until smooth like soft serve ice cream, 15 to 30 seconds. Stop processor. (Don't overmix or your ice cream will melt!)

9. Remove lid and carefully remove processor blade (ask an adult for help). Use clean rubber spatula to transfer ice cream to clean medium bowl. Place bowl in freezer. Repeat processing with remaining cubes and milk and transfer to bowl with ice cream.

10. Gently stir in pieces of cookie dough. Serve immediately. (Ice cream can be transferred to an airtight container and frozen for up to 3 days.)

~ ˈ Keep Going!

How to Measure Custard's Temperature

Pour egg yolk mixture back into saucepan with remaining cream. Whisk until well combined. Cook over low heat, stirring constantly and scraping bottom of pan with rubber spatula, until mixture thickens, registers 180 degrees on instant-read thermometer, and coats the back of a spoon, 8 to 10 minutes. (Do not let mixture come to boil.)

From Chef Ken: Keep Your Temper

Here's a surprise for you: One of the most important steps in this frozen dessert recipe involves heat. Whisking some of the hot cream into the egg yolks allows the yolks to heat up slowly, and makes sure they won't turn into solid scrambled eggs. Chefs call this technique "tempering." Once the yolks are tempered, you can add them to the rest of the hot cream mixture—they'll help thicken the custard as it cooks on the stovetop. (If you do end up with a few pieces of scrambled egg, don't worry—you'll catch them in the strainer before you freeze your ice cream base.)

MAKES enough cookie dough for 1 quart ice cream or 8 cookies
TOTAL TIME 25 minutes

beginner

Chocolate Chip Cookie Dough

For information on substituting gluten-free flours, see page 12.

Prepare Ingredients

3	tablespoons unsalted butter
¼	cup packed (1¾ ounces) brown sugar
1	tablespoon granulated sugar
1	large egg yolk (see page 16)
½	teaspoon vanilla extract
6	tablespoons (1¾ ounces) Cup4Cup Gluten-Free Multipurpose Flour
¼	teaspoon baking soda
¼	teaspoon kosher salt
¼	cup (1½ ounces) semisweet chocolate chips

Gather Cooking Equipment

▷ 10-inch skillet
▷ Rubber spatula
▷ Medium bowl
▷ Whisk

Start Cooking!

1. In 10-inch skillet, melt butter over medium-high heat. When butter is melted, reduce heat to medium-low.

2. Cook, stirring constantly and scraping bottom of pan with rubber spatula, until butter solids turn golden brown and butter smells nutty, 2 to 3 minutes. Turn off heat and carefully slide skillet to cool burner. Let browned butter cool for 2 minutes.

3. In medium bowl, whisk brown sugar, granulated sugar, egg yolk, and vanilla until combined. Carefully pour browned butter into bowl with sugar mixture (ask an adult for help—skillet will be hot), making sure to scrape out butter solids with rubber spatula. Whisk until well combined.

4. Add flour, baking soda, and salt and stir with rubber spatula until smooth. Stir in chocolate chips until combined.

5. Use your hands to pinch cookie dough into small pieces. Fold into ice cream (see step 10, page 217). (Cookie dough can be refrigerated for up to 4 days.)

TO BAKE CHOCOLATE CHIP COOKIES: In step 5, instead of pinching dough into small pieces, roll dough into 8 balls (about 1 heaping tablespoon each) and place on parchment-lined baking sheet. Place baking sheet in refrigerator and chill for 30 minutes. Bake on middle rack at 350 degrees until edges are crispy but centers are soft, 8 to 10 minutes.

Acknowledgments

This book wouldn't have been possible without all the people who have supported me as a chef, as a gluten-free eater, and as a person in general. Without their support, insight, and advice, this book wouldn't exist!

To my dad, I don't know where to begin. From the day I was born, you've been committed to two things: making my life an adventure filled with excitement and supporting me through whatever task I took on. There is no one else I would rather write a cookbook with. I love you so very much and thank you for everything you've done and continue to do for me.

To my mom, you not only gave me the idea for this book but you've also supported me every step of the way. Even more than that, you've helped me become the person I am today. You've guided me through the rough times during my diagnosis, and I know the reason I've been able to achieve writing a cookbook is all thanks to you.

To my brother, Luca, thank you for always being there for me. It means so much to me every time you try my food and film our cooking challenges. I couldn't ask for a brother who is more supportive and kind, especially with eating gluten free.

To my dog, Maple. Dogs are proven to help calm you and make you happy, and you never fail to do that for me. You're always there for me when I need a snuggle. Also, thank you for always liking my recipes.

My maternal grandparents, Minette and Papi, thank you for always asking me what I want for dinner and for teaching me how to make pesto using the herbs from your garden. I appreciate your thoughts and input as we worked on this book.

My paternal grandparents, Grannie and Bop, thank you for sharing your love of food, your constant encouragement, and most of all, for making the best mac and cheese and pancakes I'll ever have!

Brooke Elmore, thank you for helping me get used to the gluten-free lifestyle and for the best gluten-free recommendations!

Grayson Taffe, I've loved baking with you since I was little. Our recipes have often failed and made huge messes in the kitchen, but we always have fun.

Leili Singer, thank you for being the best possible friend and supporter along this journey of creating a cookbook. I can always count on you to make me laugh and make me feel comfortable.

Kevin Walsh, I spent so much time at your restaurant! Thank you for letting me make desserts with you and for teaching me so much about baking. (And thank you for introducing me to ATK Kids!)

Meghann Ward, thank you for always letting me cook with you, especially when we make doughnuts and come up with the craziest flavors. I don't think I would have had the courage to write this cookbook without all of your help.

Katy Chirichiello, thank you for showing me how to work in a restaurant kitchen and for teaching me new skills.

Monica Glass, thanks for feeding me little treats when I was at the restaurant, such as kouign amann and fondant; for helping us when we had recipe questions; and for being a great gluten-free role model.

Thank you to my pandemic second family, the Carlsons (and their dog, Comet!).

A big thank you to all my friends at school who supported me along the process.

And, of course, thank you to everyone at America's Test Kitchen Kids for bringing this cookbook to life, especially Molly Birnbaum, Suzannah McFerran, Kristin Sargianis, Ashley Stoyanov, Afton Cyrus, Andrea Wawrzyn, Faye Yang, Julie Bozzo Cote, Kevin White, Carl Tremblay, Gabi Homonoff, and Chad Chenail.

I'd like to start by thanking everyone at America's Test Kitchen Kids, especially Suzannah McFerran for her patience as we worked on these recipes and for bringing some of the seemingly impossible ideas in my mind into reality. To Molly Birnbaum, thank you for believing in our story and helping us bring it to life. And to Kristin Sargianis, thank you for the brains to put all the puzzle pieces together and for all the calm directions. I'd also like to thank the test cooks, photographers, food stylists, and photography director Julie Bozzo Cote for creating all of the beautiful photos throughout this book.

To my wife, Céline, thank you for your never-ending support and encouragement. To my daughter, Verveine, thank you for your unwavering curiosity. Working on this book has allowed us to open your mind to the treasures of everything food. Thank you for being the creative mind behind such a superfun family project. To my son, Luca, thank you for being an amazing taste tester and for always smiling. To my parents, thank you for teaching me to love food. To my teams at Uni, Toro, Coppa, Little Donkey, Faccia a Faccia, and Bar Pallino, thank you for allowing me the space to pursue interests outside of the restaurants, including this one.

Conversions and Equivalents

The recipes in this book were developed using standard U.S. measures. The charts below offer equivalents for U.S. and metric measures. All conversions are approximate and have been rounded up or down to the nearest whole number.

Volume Conversions

U.S.	METRIC
1 teaspoon	5 milliliters
2 teaspoons	10 milliliters
1 tablespoon	15 milliliters
2 tablespoons	30 milliliters
¼ cup	59 milliliters
⅓ cup	79 milliliters
½ cup	118 milliliters
¾ cup	177 milliliters
1 cup	237 milliliters
2 cups (1 pint)	473 milliliters
4 cups (1 quart)	946 milliliters
4 quarts (1 gallon)	3.8 liters

Weight Conversions

U.S.	METRIC
½ ounce	14 grams
¾ ounce	21 grams
1 ounce	28 grams
2 ounces	57 grams
3 ounces	85 grams
4 ounces	113 grams
5 ounces	142 grams
6 ounces	170 grams
8 ounces	227 grams
10 ounces	283 grams
12 ounces	340 grams
16 ounces (1 pound)	454 grams

Oven Temperatures

FAHRENHEIT	CELSIUS	GAS MARK
225°	105°	¼
250°	120°	½
275°	135°	1
300°	150°	2
325°	165°	3
350°	180°	4
375°	190°	5
400°	200°	6
425°	220°	7
450°	230°	8
475°	245°	9

Converting Temperatures from an Instant-Read Thermometer

We include doneness temperatures in some recipes in this book. We recommend an instant-read thermometer for the job. To convert a temperature from Fahrenheit to Celsius, subtract 32 from the Fahrenheit reading, and then divide the result by 1.8.

Example
"Roast chicken until thighs register 175°F."

To Convert
175°F − 32 = 143°
143° ÷ 1.8 = 79.44°C, rounded down to 79°C

Index